Love
across the
Atlantic

Love across the
Atlantic

Gweneth Jules Moorhouse

iUniverse, Inc.
Bloomington

Love Across the Atlantic

iUniverse books may be ordered through booksellers or by contacting:

iUniverse
1663 Liberty Drive
Bloomington, IN 47403
www.iuniverse.com
1-800-Authors (1-800-288-4677)

ISBN: 978-1-4759-6926-9 (sc)
ISBN: 978-1-4759-6927-6 (ebk)

Library of Congress Control Number: 2013900464

Printed in the United States of America

iUniverse rev. date: 01/11/2013

Contents

One

MOTHER

My mother was an extremely sincere, faithful, honest, very trustworthy, decent woman. She was the oldest child of five, two girls and three boys of her parents MR, and MRS. Pharoah Cuffy.

I her third child, was born in DOMINICA, Eastern Caribbean, West Indies. I did not know my father until I was seven years old. He immigrated to British Guiana, now (Guyana) In search of work when mother was pregnant with me. He had an older sister there. I therefore grew up in a single parent home with my mother and grandmother, my mother's mother.

Mother was a determined, sedate, reserved woman, busy, always working, an extremely honest, ingenuous, mind-your-own-business, never prone to gossip and idle type of woman. She was generous and very kind. She worked at all kinds of jobs to support her children. Times were changing, the population was increasing Dominica was developing. A large area of flat land in the Roseau vicinity from Pottersville to St. Aroment which was owned by the Potter family had become a vast wilderness where guava trees grew everywhere, and where everyone and anybody who had cows and sheep and goats and pigs tethered their animals. I remember Miss Potter she appeared to be of mixed heritage. She always wore wide khaki knee length shorts or khaki skirts and white long sleeve shirts. It seemed that she was the last survivor of former slave masters; she was a mulato, a boujoir. But she was now gone, housing was terrible scarce, the land was in great demand and government acquired the property to start a housing development. People purchased land and erected houses, which were springing up quickly everywhere. Sand, gravel, and stones were in great demand and mother, the industrious, enterprising woman that she was, she decided that she was going in the gravel, sand and stone business. She carried sand, gravel, stones and boulders from the beach in Fond Cole, to the roadside. From there, people who purchased these products would send huge trucks to transport these materials to their building sites.

One could easily say that most of the houses, including the Princess Margaret Hospital at the upcoming Goodwill residential area of Dominica were built from my mother's labor and sweat. Gravel, sea sand and stones etc. were in real demand. This was very lucrative business and mother worked ingenuously at capitalizing on this housing miracle. Our home was about ten minutes walk away, so before and after school, and on holidays and weekends we would help her. We filled small containers with as much as we could carry of gravel, or sand or stones, or, whichever product mother had on order for the day, and carried them from the beach a few yards away to the roadside. Mother was also engaged in other active ways, she grew a vegetable garden, reared sheep and goats, rabbits and pigs, and a cow. She kept a grocery shop and did other people's laundry. In those days all laundry were washed by hand as there were no washing machines. How mother did all these things almost all at the same time; how she worked at them all, I do not comprehend but, I never once saw her idle or heard her complain or say she was tired, she simply was indefatigable. She never had an idle moment.

As hard working as mother was, people would credit from her shop, some of them borrowed money and never repaid her, and seldom if ever, would she ask them for her money, as she thought they could not afford to repay her. She was a very special one-of-a-kind woman. She was intelligent, full of character, honesty, generosity, thoughtfulness and kindness.

Mother was beautiful inside and outside and she was very shapely too and very attractive; dark skinned with a strait pointed nose. She had an eye for industry and quality. Whatever she bought she ordered the best that her money could buy. She instructed us that it was wiser to sacrifice and buy things of quality as they lasted longer and therefore they would be cheaper in the long run. This piece of advice among the many basic and fundamental examples mother delivered to us have remained with me. I would do without anything rather than buy the cheapest one. Quality has so much more power and merit. One does not have to be rich to acquire quality. It may just call for a certain degree of self determination and sacrifice. One good product is worth its weight in durability and service against a number of less expensive products that wither and fall apart very quickly.

Mother was paying down on a plot at the housing development area when she became ill, as young as we all still were, we were incapable and unable to take charge and I presume the property was reclaimed.

I remember once mother took her gold chains earrings and bracelets to a well known, well established grocery shop owner Mr. Shand, who was godfather to my younger sister and asked him to keep her gold and give her some groceries and that she would repay him later and then she would get her items back. Mother never received her gold items for it was about that period that she became ill.

Mother never married. The fact that she never married was due to her sincerity, faithfulness and honesty to my father. She loved him dearly. She waited for him for years, his family loved her but he deceived her in the end. She was not the first woman that father must have deceived. He had a son and a daughter older than us from two different women and a daughter younger than us from yet another woman in Guyana.

When I was growing up, it was customary in the Dominican society that many people never got married. A high percentage of the population of men and women lived together for years without getting married and raised their children as normal happy families. It was always a concern to me that my grandparents, both my father's and my mother's parents were married, and my parents were not. Though we were very happy children, I felt a void in my family and sometimes I was ashamed that there was no father in my home. I realized that was the reason my mother was over burdened working so hard to maintain her children.

I remember a well established well endowed estate owner, a neighbor, who knew my mother very well, Miss Florrie Jolly called me aside one day and explained to me that besides it all and the situation that my mother had found herself in, that we should always respect her for she has always been a very hard working, honest and respectful person and she wanted us to know that. I was proud to know that folks recognized the real characteristics of my mother. She definitely was a woman of high standards.

Father visited us in Dominica, when I was seven years old, that's when I first met him, my two elder sisters, Beatrice was eleven 11, and Sonia, was 9. We formed our opinions of him and we really never warmed up to him.

I must have been about nine or ten and it became apparent that mother was not well, I was cleaning the home and I seized the opportunity to clean and rearrange her bureau (dresser) which really was off limits to us, and what do you think? Stocked away in a corner, way in the back of the inside of the bureau was a package perfectly wrapped and stuffed into a pillow case well hidden away. I found what was undoubtedly my mother's most cherished possession "letters from my father," I read each one of them, full with his empty promises to marry my mother. I related the news to my sisters and I destroyed each, every single letter, all of them, without mother's permission or knowledge. She no doubt thought that her precious letters were still in their secrete apartment, for she NEVER asked for them.

From that day, I made up my mind that no man was going to get my back on the ground, impregnate me and walk away, then to leave me with the obligation, and all it entails of, supporting, and raising his children alone, then to marry another woman. I determined that that wasn't going to happen to me so I had to be strong in combat against the boys.

Father appeared very gentlemanly but he really was a scoundrel. Why, even for his children's sake would he treat my mother and us like this? He never sent anything to us and he had the audacity to have named my oldest sister "Beatrice" after his sister and to name me, whom he had not ever seen, "Edricka" after his older brother Federick. This proves the degree to which my mother emulated, loved and respected him. When he returned to Dominica, he was residing at the home of his oldest daughter's mother—???—What in the world made that man so endearing to women? He alone knows, but, they all loved him. Love him as they did, he must have sensed our resentment towards him, my sisters and I we never warmed up to him and after perhaps one year or so later, he moved to Barbados where he had two older sisters. He was the youngest of six; three boys, three girls, and they all babied him.

Father worked as an agriculturist in Barbados. He later married a Barbadian woman who had one adult son who immigrated to England. Father and his wife had no children together but his oldest daughter Hermia, at whose home he stayed on his return from Guyana, whether or not he was her sponsor, to Barbados, she lived with father and his wife.

Mother, an attractive a female as she was, now that my father was married, and perhaps in trying to obtain affection for herself and assistance in providing for her three children, she had an admirer whom she fell in love with and they had two daughters. She worked steadfastly, and incessantly, to support them. She raised sheep, goats, rabbits and pigs and a cow. My two elder sisters and I tended the animals we were called shepherds by our schoolmates because every morning and afternoon we had to transfer the cow, the sheep and the goats from the Pottersville Savannah or the New Town Savannah to and from our home on Bath Road. Roseau is a small town, now called the capital city. Fortunately, our home was equidistant between the two savannahs north and south of Roseau, neither was far away. The cow was slaughtered for sale. The pigs and rabbits were kept at Kings Hill, and after school we had to carry the breadfruits, and green banana peels and dasheen skins that we cooked to the pigs and fetch vines for the rabbits. It was no use complaining, the animals had to be fed and mother insisted that we fed them, and, it really was great fun caring for and playing with the animals. We had a jolly good time and we loved the animals. Anytime either a sheep, or a goat, even the pig would pull itself loose, they would all find their way home. Residents all knew to whom they belonged, and no one ever disturbed any of them.

Mother's first cousin Mrs. Peter, her husband, and family lived at Kings Hill which, at that time, was a government agricultural station with acres of open ground and no other dwelling houses. Our cousins were the overseers. They were good to us and we had fun playing with their children.

Dominica was in a real state of development, at that period, new laws were being implemented and it became unlawful to take sand, gravel and stones out from the beach, that which was by far the biggest lump of mother's income, but, the busy body that she was, and, having five girls to support she would not loiter.

MR HART

Long before we realized anything, mother had become the housekeeper of Mr. Thomas Clifford Hart, a retired Welchman, for whom she had worked before, and whose laundry she was still doing. She was the only helper and Mr. Hart trusted her c o m p l e t e l y. He lived alone in an extremely extensive "L" shaped wooden house at Elms Hall, the only house at that time in a big scenic valley. MR. Hart was a bachelor, and he always dressed in white light cotton short sleeve shirts without collars, and white cotton tie-waist long pants, he wore soft shoe loafers(I can see him now,) He was tall, and handsome, slight to medium built with striking blue eyes. He was always reading and never left his home compound. The furthest I knew that he would go, was to walk to his tennis court. A sparsely used public dirt road separated the house from the tennis court. That house was ideally located in the valley beneath Morne Bruce, amid acres and acres of lemon trees, owned by L. ROSE & Company. They had a large complex at Bath Estate with huge pressing machines where they extracted the lemon juice and lime juice which were exported around the world. The lemon trees were the only other inhabitants of the valley, there was hardly anyone around except when day laborers came to gather the lemons and weed the fields. Coming from the Roseau direction, a dirt road to the left led to more lemon trees, acres and more acres of them, and then down to the Roseau River. This valley was very scenic and peaceful, a place of birds, butterflies and bees, quiet and serene, in solace and scientific imaginings, a truly healthy wholesome, beautiful place.

Traveling to or from Trafalgar, Laudat, and Wotten Waven all in the Roseau Valley, one could see this sprawling wooden house far across from the river, the only building in that large picturesque, scenic valley. That is the environment in which we grew up, happy and content, abiding, respectful and dutifully engaged. We had to be, you see Mr. Hart made us feel comfortable, in fact he was like a father to us and very generous.

Mother had early instilled into our heads, the values of honesty.

"You might find money all over the place, on the floor, on the shelves, in the cupboards, anywhere" mother instructed us "if you pick it up, hand it to Mr. Hart, if you think you do not want to hand it to him, leave it exactly where you find it" mother said to us, and that is exactly how it was we never kept one cent.

Mr. Hart owned a large estate at Mount Luke where he kept his most valuable possessions, that place was beautifully furnished and stocked with all kinds of expensive things and goodies,

English cookies, English biscuits and McIntosh toffees and other special things that I never saw in the shops in Roseau.

On school vacations he would furnish the place with groceries, mother had the keys, and we spent our holidays at the estate. We walked from Roseau to mount Luke a distance of over ten miles quite many times as vehicles were very few in those days, Mr. Hart very seldom came there. He never had a vehicle anyway. To us walking to Mount Luke was part of the fun for we knew good times awaited us there. We helped to keep the place clean and we had the times of our lives. We roamed in and out of that big beautiful wooden mansion, we romped and frolicked on the large green lawns and swung on swings which were hung on a huge tree. There was a watchman who overlooked the place, milked the cows, brought milk to Mr. Hart, attended the lawns and mowed and kept them in perfect order. He hunted birds for us which we roasted over a fire. We had great fun. A few hundred yards from the main house, was a well designed cottage where mother lived in what must have been servant quarters of slave masters, former owners of the estate and mansion house. At the cottage we would skim the cream off the milk into a class churner and churned it to butter fresh homemade butter. We had so much more milk than we could consume. We were tired of milk. We added water and fresh cinnamon, sometimes we added eggs, bay leaves, and other varied spices to afford us different flavors, we were so tired of milk, we wished mother would give milk to other folks, but, there too, was a very private place with no neighbors, and though mother had friends and relatives, as far as she was concerned, the milk was not hers, so it was not her privilege to give it away she therefore asked the watchman that he should milk the cows less often.

Mr. Hart had good friends who visited him regularly at Elms Hall, the Dupigny brothers and Mr. Dewhurst. They were married with children, but I never saw neither their wives nor their children come to Elms Hall or Mount Luke. We previously thought MR. Dewhurst was a bachelor also, but years later we discovered that he was married to a local woman and they had several children. The last was a boy much darker than all the others, he had his mother's complexion but he was his father's shadow, almost every where MR. Dewhurst went, you would find the shadow following. When I grew up and was married many, many years later, my husband purchased Moore Park we discovered that MR. Dewhurst owned a beautiful property in Bourne about three miles south of Moore Park.

Mr. Hart raised land turtles as pets, and chickens for eggs and consumption, in fact he owned the chickens but mother and we girls raised them, every week we bought corn by the bags-full and by the bushels from produce vendors at the Old Roseau Market, now the Tourist Vendors Market. It was fun and we had a good sense of obligation and responsibility. We fed the chickens and collected the eggs every day.

Mother taught us by example, she knew her place and her boundaries and she would not over-step them, neither could we. For all the many years we were at Elms Hall I never knew that there was a swimming pool built into the basement, below the large dinning room, till I was well grown up. Mother cleaned that area herself, and she always kept those doors locked. Being a very devoted, dedicated, attentive, concerned mother, of course she well knew that girls could be inquisitive and could get into the wrong places and at the wrong times. She set the boundaries of where we were allowed to go and where we weren't. We had no problems complying with her standards. We had a jolly, jolly, good time and we were very happy indeed.

But mother was no longer well, she could not work; my oldest sister had to take over the reigns. She was employed at The Convent Industrial School where they made grass rugs, bags and hats from local straw. The other four of us were still students. Life was now difficult, money was extremely scarce.

Beatrice had a bright idea. She bought some straw and began making a rug at home after work. On completion, she took the rug to MR. Hart and asked him to buy it. He thought it was beautiful and artistic so he bought it, no questions asked. We were overjoyed. From that day on, at intervals when our needs were in demand, we helped Beatrice sew rugs and we brought them to MR. Hart. Never once did he reject, nor refuse. That good man must have sensed our need and anytime we went to him with a rug be assured that he bought the rug and he would let us place them where we decided. That was the nature of the man.

GRANDMOTHER

During school times we were at our grandmother, my mother's mother, mama Pharoah was a wonderful person and a splendid grandmother, she was a great disciplinarian, but she was absolutely very kind and generous, not only to us but to everybody and anybody. Almost everyone knew her or had heard about her. They knew her name and exactly who she was. Her husband Mr. Pharoah Cuffy was from a very well known family from River Cyricque. There were very few roads and fewer still, almost no vehicles in Dominica at the time. On the East Coast, walking, no matter how far one had to go was the mode life. There were few vehicular roads and no vehicles. Coming to Roseau meant people had to walk long distances through the night on Fridays from La Plaine, Rosalie, Grand Fond, and other villages, all through CHEME' LETANG (Lake Road) to Laudat and then on and on to Roseau, so people from the east and surrounding villages when they came to Roseau, many of them stayed at my grandmother's. I well remember as a little girl growing up that every week end we always had lots of company with people sleeping all over our floors on Friday and Saturday nights. Every available space would be occupied. I can, in my mind's eye, see them now. Saturdays, at the Roseau Market, they would sell produce, coffee, corn, ground provisions, bananas, live chickens, eggs, etc. etc. and whatever else they brought, then they purchased commodities like rice, sugar, soap, butter, pots and pans and other items they needed, and on Sundays, before we awoke, they would have gone, all of them gone with their parcels and boxes and kerosene stoves, and cloth, and shoes and whatever else that they had bought. Gone on their long haul of a journey, walking back home.

We had two small houses facing each other north to south. The larger was my grandmother's, the smaller, my mother's. There was one large kitchen for the family, which, before I was born, was a cow-pen where my grandmother milked her cows. A huge avocado tree which bore very big, luscious red skin fruits when ripe, grew from inside the converted kitchen, an outlet was cut so the tree branched out into the open. Elsewhere on the property, there was a big kennip tree, a papaw tree, and a sugar-apple tree.

I loved to climb the trees so I was always the one picking the fruits. I was by no means a tom-boy. I just liked climbing the trees. There was no boy in the family to climb them. I was a very stylish girl, and popular with the boys, they always came home, sometimes when I saw certain ones coming that I didn't care for too much, I hid away and sometimes ran in at one door of one house and go out at another unnoticed. One day a group of them were home asking for me, my grandmother had seen enough of this, she was curious, she confronted me head on, she opened her big brown eyes directly into mine and in serious, determined, controlling fashion questioned me in our native Creole, "mois le' konnet qui le dayoo? ("I want to know, your mind, what are you up to?") My grandmother was something to behold, she was everything to us while my mother worked. Growing up in those environments we did, we were very happy and well cared for.

We were very popular and talented girls if I must say. There was a tall, big kennip tree on our property. My granduncle's house was next door, there were high wooden steps erected close to the Kennip tree in the direction of our front door. We decided we were going to stage concerts based on certain things we learnt in school, poems, and civics especially. We made costumes from our mother's and grandmother's clothes and memorized our parts. We decorated the steps as a stage and erected a bench beneath the kennip tree. We invited our friends in the evenings and took to the stage. Our friends were very amazed and they wanted to partake of the fun in future plays. News about our concerts spread, and soon adults were joining in the audience which they too enjoyed. Before very long our concerts became a real phenomenon and every month we staged concerts at moonlight time and we all, adults and school girls had real entertainment and great amusement. We were much congratulated for our efforts. We also played ring games and people came from their neighborhoods to watch our concerts, play ring games and join in the fun. That made us very proud indeed.

Grandmother's sister Aunty Baby was another factor of joy and happiness in our lives. She had no children. She worked at Morne Daniel, Rockaway and Canefield Estates which all belonged to Mr. Daniel Green's father. The properties adjoined each other and formed a very extensive place which was all planted with limes and sugar cane. On holidays and weekends weed helped Aunty Baby to collect limes. There were lots of grafted mango and bitter skin mango trees everywhere. Aunty Baby informed us very early on that we could eat all the mangoes we could but it was estate orders that no mangoes were to be carried away. We of course abided by the rule. Aunty Baby was a share cropper. As a share cropper she had the privilege of growing sugar cane on a plot for herself. At cane cutting time we rushed home from school and hurried to Morne Daniel where her plot was. We ate sugarcane and mangoes all day long as we rushed back and forth carrying sugarcane bundles. We carried the canes which were tied into bundles from the field to the roadside, an estate truck would collect the canes and take them to factory where the canes would be crushed into juice and made into rum and other products. The profits were calculated on a share or subsistence basis with Mr. Green.

We had fun all throughout the day and never had a dull moment. At lunchtime Aunty Baby would go for mangoes, she had a method where she would roll her skirt up, gather it at the hemline, full it up with mangoes and carry them to us. She dug yams from her yam patch and cooked the yams over an open wood fire. Those fresh yams were as white and soft and as delicious as you could get; the best yams we ever had.

On Friday afternoons we would go with Aunty Baby to "LA COO" (the big yard) at Canefield to get her pay for the week. That place must have been a center of much commercial activity in the days of slavery when slaves worked on the sugarcane and lime fields. That's the place where the "MILL" or grinding wheel was; that's where the sugar cane was pressed, that's where the limes were squeezed. There Aunty Baby would get "VISOO" (crush sugarcane juice) this fresh squeezed cane juice was a great treat for us and we always looked forward to that time.

The old sugarcane grinding place is now "The Old Mill Cultural Center" where cultural events are staged. Young writers, actors, artists, and other individuals try out their skills and keep their performances.

Rockaway is now a manufacturing and commercial center, while Morne Daniel and the rest of Canefield are housing development areas.

A portion of Canefield Estate is where the Canefield Airport is located. This was the first airport on Dominica. It provided links to and from Dominica and the outside world.

As business developed at the airport and traffic grew, there was need for a bigger more updated airport and the Melville Hall Airport was built. This airport is about one hour's ride from the City of Roseau and though driving through to Roseau affords majestic scenic views of nature in all peaceful splendor, many business people and some local folk prefer to travel in and out of the Canefield Airport which is only ten minutes from the capital.

AUNT EUNICE

Mother had three brothers and one sister, her brothers all had families of their own, her only sister, Aunt Eunice was unmarried, she had no children. She lived in Aruba. She immigrated to Aruba when I was three years old. If ever there was a blessed angel, if ever there was a spirited angel born, it had to be my Aunt Eunice. We her sister's five daughter's, helping us was her greatest concern, and helping us she did in very fundamental ways. She was outstanding. She was a miracle. She was the provider my father neglected to be. She was the light God shone over us. She was always sending parcels to us in Dominica. Everything one could buy for food or clothing, Aunt Eunice sent to us, by air, by boat, by friends by acquaintances, any way she could, as often as she had the opportunity to do so. She sent parcels filled with, dolls, toys, pencils, books, dresses, shoes, socks, toilet soaps, laundry soaps, cereal, cooking oil, oatmeal, biscuits, candies etc. etc. You name it, whatever money could buy, came to us in Dominica through the post office, the customs office, on boats, on airplanes, and in peoples' bags and boxes. I remember the largest and biggest dictionary that I have ever seen, a huge Webster's Dictionary with indented alphabetical edges, commodities of various assortments which Aunt Eunice bought in Aruba and sent to us in Dominica, and money too of course. In addition to all this, she took it upon herself to pay for my older sister's high school education. I remember Aunt Eunice sent to us a glass and wood clothes wash board which we never received. Many, many, many years later I went to the customs building to collect some goods which I had ordered, and as I looked across the room, over yonder, there on a box, I saw a wash board. I went closer to examine the thing, and sure enough, my grandmother's name was written on that truant washboard awaiting a homecoming. I remember too what I think was the last parcel from Aunty Eunice, a parcel specifically for my youngest sister's confirmation. She had never ever met Joyce, but Joyce was her sister's youngest daughter and she was going to receive the sacrament of confirmation so a parcel arrived by mail, a beautiful white dress, a white veil, a pair of white gloves, a pair of white shoes and a pair of white socks and white underwear. Everything, dress up and go. Though she had never met, nor seen our youngest sister Joyce. There simply was no limit to what Aunt Eunice did for us. She provided us with everything, all the time. There just could not be another aunt as dedicated as my Aunt Eunice. I often wonder how she knew our sizes because when she left Dominica my oldest sister Beatrice, was seven, Sonia was 5, I was three, Myrtle was a baby and, Joyce was not yet born. Aunt Eunice, She had not ever returned to Dominica but she was always there in the hearts of her five nieces, and also in her heart and soul. As children, we well realized we were very fortunate in so many ways, we used to say "We have three mothers, one who works to provide our daily needs and every day food, one who takes care of us, washes our clothes and corrects us, and one who supplies our clothes, shoes, toys, school supplies and much, much more. Aunt Eunice was just indispensable, indescribable, her generosity cannot be surpassed; she was giving, thoughtful, kind, dedicated, generous and loving. We were especially fortunate to have such kind and loving folks whose characteristics we inherited. Their marks on our lives cannot be erased. Their selflessness and Godly manner, their character and feelings for their neighbors, their examples are with us as we strive to be of service to others.

When I grew up and was living in the USA I had the good fortune and opportunity to have Aunt Eunice come visit. I felt this was the least I could have done for her in appreciation for the life she spent being a father in providing for us. Later after I got married and was living in Moore Park, Dominica, I purchased a caravan house for her that the Canadians who worked on a road building project had for sale at the completion of their project; unfortunately, she did not want to reside in Moore Park and much to my contrary, she returned to Aruba which had been her home for as long as I knew her. Regretfully Aunty Eunice passed away there days before her neighbors realized she was missing. I have the consolation that I had made it my duty, Sonia and I, to have visited her in Aruba a few years before she passed. Sonia too had a small house on a property she purchased at Copt Hall which she offered to Aunt Eunice, but Aruba had become her home and there she returned

SCHOOL TIME

We were Catholics and we attended Catholic elementary school. That was free. My grandmother told me when my two elder sisters would leave for school that I would cry all day long so she finally asked the school principal to allow her to send me along which they did. There was no kindergarten no nursery schools in those days. We attended the Convent Primary School, renamed St. Martin's School. I recall when I was nine years old and in standard one which was the biggest room and at the corner, the center of the big "L" shaped building, I was finished with my class assignment and was then reading a story; there was a mishap in class to which I was paying no attention, the teacher blamed me for the goings on; I tried to convince her without success that I knew nothing about the matter but she continued to blame me and took my book away which she placed on her desk; in retaliation, I took my book; well she reported me to the principal who asked to see my grandmother; I re-affirmed that I knew not what the contention was about, however, I was reprimanded for taking my book off the teacher's desk and all seemed well, however, at the end of the school year I had skipped standard two and was promoted to standard three. In standard three, my teacher Miss Erica Shillingford, turned out to be the teacher I most loved and admired throughout my school life. Her astuteness, her diligence, and deportment reminded me of my mother. She was an excellent teacher. Towards the end of the school year, right before prize giving ceremonies, Miss Shillingford called me to her desk and asked me to pick one of two folded pieces of paper which she had placed in a hat, after I chose one, she asked me to open the paper, written thereon, was *Gweneth Jules* at the prize giving ceremony, I received the prize for 'steady application' and I was promoted from standard three to standard five. At thirteen years old, I was in the senior class, standard seven, and, anytime a teacher would be sick or absent, the principal would have my class teacher send me to take the class. It filled me with great pride, honor and much delight. In the senior class you had to take the School Leaving Examination; I did; and I was successful, but I remained in the senior class till I was fifteen and a half years old. This means I sat the School Leaving Examinations three times. I was successful each time. I kept on going to school; nobody stopped me. I was too young to leave school and there was no money to send me to the Convent High School which you had to pay to attend. My older sister Sonia was a student there. When I was fifteen and a half the school principal, Sister Mary Borgia recruited me as a "Pupil-Teacher," I received no pay, three months later, I was appointed by government; my pay or salary :—five shillings a month—(US$2.34). At that time Dominica was still a British possession, hence, we used British currency. During this period, teachers received no formal training, the brightest students were recruited as pupil teachers and they studied and were administered yearly examinations. Those who failed, were dismissed, those who were successful were promoted to a higher level. I never, ever failed. I reached all levels and taught every class or grade level in the Dominica elementary school system. I was Pupil Teacher, Probationary Teacher, Assistant Teacher, all except School Principal. At twenty six years of age I was Assistant Teacher, next in line to being School Principal. I was then transferred to a Canada sponsored newly built and just opening Goodwill Junior High School, from there I was transferred to Trafalgar Government School, next in authority after the principal. I petitioned the education Department against this transfer from the Roseau area since I was the only bread winner responsible for, and taking care of my aging grandmother, my sick mother, who had worked extremely hard, and my youngest sister, eight years my junior. I could ill afford to pay rent or boarding never-the-less buying a vehicle on the pittance I was receiving. The Education Officers did not grant my request so the alternative was to walk to Trafalgar about seven miles rain or shine and walk back home in the evenings unless I received a ride from a Good Samaritan. I walked many, times till I noticed an Education officer who knew who I was, and where I was going, drive up my direction going to the school where I was stationed or to other schools in the surrounding area ; he was not kind nor humanitarian enough to offer or give me a ride. Well that was too much. As dedicated a teacher as I was, and who used my meager salary to buy school supplies, and food and sometimes clothing for needy students, I made up my mind that as long as I got a ride that I would go to Trafalgar, and that I would wait at the junction to Trafalgar "untill and if" I got a ride and that if I got no ride, I would return to my home. Well the said Education Officer passed me standing by a few times more; he must have noticed also that I did not show up at the Trafalgar Government School and realized he passed and saw me standing by. Two weeks afterwards, I was transferred to the New Town Infant Boys School in the Roseau vicinity. I was a hard working, very dedicated primary School Teacher in Dominica, and I had become known as one of the best. I really poured my whole self into teaching, I loved it and I gave it all I had. I would think of different ways in which I could impress those young minds, their learning and performance was my responsibility. I took children home and helped those who needed assistance with their school work, those who lacked proper care and those who needed supplies. This was very rewarding to me.

It is often said "what comes around goes around"

Happenings and events do come and go around. They do shape our character and determine what kind of persons we become, in manners and in places, and with persons and at times that we least expect.

Four of my most rewarding moments of being a school teacher are:-

(1) After efforts at taming a notorious pre-teen student were almost exhausted, the principal sent her to my class as a class member, She was from a very poor family of ten children, she was rough and ready, inattentive and boisterous and she had little respect for rule and order, the kind of person who was always in trouble of one kind or another. One day soon after, she was enrolled in my class, she came to class with a stack of

various new school supplies, and other items. I knew immediately that something strange was in the making. I called her to my desk and questioned her, letting her know that I expected the truth and nothing less. I informed her just what her punishment would be if she didn't. She answered my questions straightforwardly and truthfully and told me that she had stolen the items from Astaphan's shopping center, ironically, apart from being a teacher. I was a longtime part-time employee at Astaphan's, the largest department store in Dominica. I asked the student to take all the items and return them to the managing director, apologize for stealing them, and to bring me back a note signed personally by him. Before very long, the student was walking back, smiling, I knew straight away that she had done what I asked her to do and that she felt pride within herself. On her arrival she handed me a note signed by the director and she beamed a broad smile, I hugged and congratulated her, gave her a kiss on the cheek and asked her to take her seat. She walked away in a positive manner and I knew that we both had accomplished a great mission. From that day on I noticed a tremendous change in that student and I thanked God for it.

(2) One day I was explaining Arithmetic to the class and I was interrupted several times by a student who kept on talking to her neighbor, that student was not as efficient in Arithmetic as she could have been, so after several warnings, I informed her that I had enough of her talking, and that she should not allow me to find her talking again, well talking again she was, she was talking again, I called her and stood her against a huge closet close to my desk. I pulled the door ajar and I

continued my lesson, she could hear me but she could not see the other students. The news reached her mother who came to me after lunch break, I explained to her what the situation was, we discussed the problem, the lady reprimanded her daughter, thanked me, and left. This student really curtailed her endless talking habit, her Arithmetic improved steadily, she went on to High School, then on to college, and she became the Principal of the Dominica Seventh Day Adventist Secondary School where two of my sons were attending. Meantime, her mother and I grew in deep respect and admiration of each other, the young lady immigrated to the U.S.A, She became a Psychologist and whenever she would be visiting the island, she would come visit me.

(3) Once I took a trip to Antigua to sell Produce which I harvested from my agricultural estate. I had no personal contacts in Antigua but I was extremely confident that I would manage fine. On arriving at the market, I approached the market vendors informing them that I had produce for sale, some of them were immediately interested, some were hesitant, perhaps of doing business with a stranger, but I persevered, while I was attending to a would be client whom it appears wanted to beat my prices, a young woman who ran a snack bar directly across the street from the market was watching the proceedings from her doorway, she walked towards me and called me by name in earnest, "Miss Jules" she said, excitedly, "Don't let anyone beat you down, let them know that you were my teacher and they are not going to have things their way." Having said those words, she took over and remained with me till every item was sold. I then inquired of her information about

getting a reasonably priced guesthouse. "Miss Jules," She uttered, "guesthouse? Do you forget the times you used to take me to your home, comb my hair, and feed me? You are not going to any guest house. I want you to come home with me. I just moved into a brand new house, there is plenty room for you." We walked across to her snack bar, she served me lunch, we talked about times past and later she took me to her beautiful new home in a suburb of St. John's, she catered to me hands and foot till I was ready to leave, she would not accept one cent from me, instead she reiterated that I had been very good to her and patient, when she was a student. I thanked her for her kindness and generosity, I congratulated her for her achievements, she wished me a safe trip, volunteered that I was free and welcome to return anytime, and I left for the airport.

(4) I was a teacher while my older sister Sonia was still a student at the Convent High School. My mother was sick and unable to work. Money was scarce. Sonia had to sit the Fifth Form Qualifying Examinations administered by Cambridge University of England which had to be paid for in advance. On the meager salary I received, I walked confidently to the Roseau Credit Union and applied for a loan. I was a credit union member while a student, and I had transferred whatever little savings I had to the Roseau Credit Union; I explained the situation, the reason I was there. With precious little hesitation of a doubt; I walked out with the money I requested as happy as anyone could ever be. After Sonia graduated, she was employed at ST. Martin's School where I was teaching, we were on the same grade level; Sonia was shortly thereafter

assigned to the same classroom where I was stationed, the class enrollment was one hundred two (102) girls, among the students were our youngest sister Joyce, and our first cousin Margaret. I had been an elementary school teacher since I was fifteen and one half years old; before that, as a student at thirteen and fourteen years of age, I was often called upon to take the class of any teacher who was absent, much to my self esteem, pride, enjoyment and delight.

I worked extremely hard and developed programs and methods of grasping the students' interest and involvement in school work. Their progress, achievement and success were my responsibility.

THE GENTLEMAN FROM NORTON

One day in 1966 a gentleman from Norton, Massachusetts a tourist, was living at Cherry Lodge Hotel in the center of Roseau. It was carnival time, as custom goes, bands of people, young and old dancing to loud, local calypso music, take to the streets in colorful costumes, fully covered or scantily dressed, however they wished, except bareness or full outright nakedness. People wore masks and some carried sticks or machetes as signs of power. The Gentleman from Norton, from his hotel, heard and saw a thick band of revelers approaching, unaccustomed to all this, the man was scared and he thought the folks were coming after him. He soon had relief to learn that the revelers were harmless and that they were only participating in carnival and enjoying themselves in the yearly festival.

The following day the man walked into Astaphan's Shopping Center and ordered a cold drink. Apart from being a school teacher, I had worked part time at Astaphan's for years on school and public holidays and on weekends.

The gentleman approached the cash register where I was stationed, to pay for his drink; we struck into a conversation, before we concluded, I asked him. "What is the easiest and quickest way to gain entry into the U.S.A?" Like a walking encyclopedia, the Gentleman from Norton listed a full page of college and university names with their addresses, he wrote his name and address, handed me the paper while he said to me, "write to these schools, and write to me so I can recommend you."

I had one specific reason in mind for wanting to go to the USA. A young man who was born in Dominica, and grew up in Aruba had come to Dominica with his Dominican parents together with my Aunt Eunice, they visited us and Augustus and I became attracted to each other, but he and his family returned to Aruba shortly after, from Aruba he immigrated to England, we corresponded for a few years and he wanted me to join him in England, since I was the only working person at home at that time I decided that I couldn't go. I did not go. Meantime, Augustus immigrated to Dorchester, Massachusetts, USA and he again wished that I could join him. My youngest sister Joyce was now employed so I was eager and wanted to go. I wrote to several of the schools in the USA and I wrote to the gentleman, shortly afterwards I received a letter from the Gentleman From Norton; we continued to correspond with each other and noticing that both the gentleman and my boyfriend Augustus were in Massachusetts, I asked of each of them how far Dorchester was from Norton and whether they could get in touch with each other. Neither of them remarked about that.

Meanwhile, the colleges which replied to me were asking for high school diploma and proof of other kinds of qualifications which I did not have. I relayed this to the Gentleman from Norton; he immediately filed immigration papers on my behalf, and got me an offer of employment in the USA.

Meantime, for three consecutive years, I had been trying to immigrate to Canada on The Canada/Dominica Domestic Scheme, and for three consecutive years I was left out while other girls I helped were recruited. In disgust I wrote directly to the Canadian Immigration Department. I received a very favorable reply within two-and-one-half weeks stating that they would be delighted to have me come to Canada, for I was brilliant and they remarked that I wrote a very interesting letter. I was informed that a Canadian Officer would come to interview me in Dominica, the time and date and place for the interview were stated. The interviewer came exactly as scheduled, after a few questions the officer stated that they certainly, definitely would be happy to have me in Canada. He then inquired whether I could afford to pay the passage money to Canada, I replied that I did not have the money presently but I was certain that I could get it even if I had to take a loan, "Never mind taking a loan," The officer said to me, quickly, as though he was anticipating such a response. "I will advance you the passage money, and when you get to Canada, you will pay us back how much you can, when you can, free of interest," I could hardly believe my ears. Did I hear correctly? Was I dreaming? Was I hoping? No! I absolutely, most definitely, was not hoping, nor was I dreaming. The kind thoughtful, analyzing, decisive, humanitarian, immediately signed a check and handed it to me, along with other necessary documents I would need for legal entrance into Canada. He wished me well. I thanked him for his goodness, kindness and generosity. I was on my way happy, excited and full of anticipation as ever as I had ever experienced before.

Meantime, the gentleman from Norton and I continued with our correspondence, he made several visits to Dominica and each time he came he would hire a car, and come home to visit. He loved to go around Dominica exploring. Every time I would be free, he invited me along. We toured the island. It was mango season, the man loved mangoes, and mangoes grew everywhere. The ground was littered yellow with ripe mangoes; he ate and ate. Once we came across a huge cashew tree with red ripe cashew plums. I think it was the first time he had ever seen a cashew tree. The tree was tall and the ground was covered with red, ripe, just fallen cashew plums with their nuts affixed. That to him was a new experience. He was excited and he sucked on one cashew plum after another. He then broke a few cashew seeds open; and my goodness! They say ignorance is bliss! Yes I witnessed how disastrous, how damaging ignorance can be. Not knowing how potent cashew-nut-oil can be, and, before I could stop him, the great adventurer that he is, this tall handsome man, noticing the oils from the cashew nuts on both his hands, he rubbed his face and bald hair spot, vigorously, thinking perhaps that he had found nature's purest body and face lotion. Within a little while his face reddened and soon the skin began to peel of his face here and there and off his forehead. But, would a tall grown up man cry in the presence of a young innocent woman whose company he sought? He took it all in stride scald forehead, scaled patchwork face and all, he swallowed his manly pride and he remained calm and focused on enjoying himself. We did, we had a marvelous time. I bet he'd never forget his cashew adventure.

At the Windsor Park, that is many, many years long before the stadium was built, it was habitual that my friends and other groups of young women played competitive netball there. Every day morning and afternoon before and after school I would be practicing. The man would come every afternoon to the Windsor Park, he watched us play, and he remained till I was finished and ready to go.

I was a very keen and popular player and had lots of fans. I was twice selected to the Dominica team which played in Caribbean Netball Tournaments. My first national exposure was the time the Caribbean Tournament was held in Dominica. My second exposure was the following year 1963 when the tournament was held in Trinidad and Tobago and I was a hit on the field from my first game, fans flocked around me much to the envy and discontent of some girls on my team. People do not realize how some women grudge those who are more popular with the opposite sex than they are. Young men were calling and visiting the guesthouse where we stayed, several of them were interested in meeting me. We were at a party hosted by the Prime Minister of Trinidad and Tobago he too held a conversation with me. This all turned the tide into a subtle rebellion against me, and I was replaced on the team by the standby, the reserved player and players would attend team social activities without informing me so often I was left at the guesthouse alone. Fortunately, the guesthouse was owned and run by Dominicans so I had companion to pass the time away.

Soon meantime, I received papers from the American Embassy in Bridgetown, Barbados, informing me that I should report to Barbados for the signing of my visa to the U.S.A, the date and time having been affixed. When I reported to Barbados, I did not receive the visa but I was told that a document which should have been put in my file was misplaced and I was informed that I would get the visa very shortly thereafter. I returned home determined to make immediate plans to leave for Canada. "When God is with you, no one can be against you."

Canada and Dominica have always maintained very friendly Diplomatic Relations, they are both former British possessions, both are now independent countries, both are members of the British Commonwealth of Nations, and they both speak English and a French Creole. In 1967 when Canada celebrated its 100th Anniversary of Independence the Canadian Government decided to double the increase in the quota of the number of ladies it would allow to immigrate to Canada that year on the Canada-Dominica Domestic Scheme. Dominica therefore selected all the girls who had received the training previously but who were not selected.

T H I S W A S M Y M O M E N T, t h e r e w a s n o h o l d i n g m e b a c k a n y m o r e

I-was-one-of-those-girls. The irony though is that I no longer needed it, it was a wasted slot since I could not pass it on to someone else. There was no one trained left. I now had two documented, valid legal entrance opportunities to immigrate to Canada, and an American Visa soon to be had, all at that moment in time. I was more than thrilled and excited. I was ecstatic. I was sitting on top of the world to greener pastures, personal development, and a better life. I set my departure date for May 14, 1967.

I decided I was moving to Canada closer to the USA. I would not wait. As happy though I was, I was overwhelmed by the fact that I had three legal, documented ways to seek a better education, advancement and affluence which young Dominicans so ardently crave and I did not have the where-with-all to dispense the other two opportunities to requiring, needy, wanting, individuals. That, was a sincere and genuine burden on me, it haunted me. How I wished that laws, could have been mended so I could be permitted to extend the two unused opportunities to two other girls. As an independent immigrant to Canada, I was free to seek employment anywhere, while on the Domestic Scheme the girls would be assigned as household helpers.

On May 7, 1967 the gentleman from Norton visited Dominica, purpose: to wish me a safe passage to North America; to wish me a pleasant time in Canada; to say goodbye in person; and most especially and specifically he said; to say that he had fallen in love with me. He left three days before my departure.

Seven

Living in Canada

On May 14, 1967 when I disembarked the airplane after my arrival at Toronto International Airport, my girlfriend Janet, who was my neighbor I grew up with and whom I had helped with the requisites for selection on the scheme to Canada; was at the airport to meet me, so was the gentleman from Norton. I had the greatest surprise of my life. He never mentioned that he would come, he had driven all the way from Norton, Massachusetts in a large white two door Pontiac Bonneville, all alone, all the way to Toronto, to give me a surprise: to welcome me to North America. THAT was very emotional and exciting, indeed. I was thrilled, happy, and enthralled in the moment. That was extra special. We parted that night and he promised to come early in the morrow. That day he drove me around Toronto, the following day he drove me through some suburbs of Toronto and to the home of his friends in Willowdale. Friends he knew very well, an insurance agent and his wife who were transferred from Attleboro, Massachusetts to Canada. He left the following day.

The next weekend, my second in Toronto, Augustus came to visit me, and so it was, two week-ends in Toronto, two male visitors, both from Massachusetts, the gentleman from Norton, and the young man Augustus from Dorchester, both proclaiming their love for me. I was in the center of a three edged love affair, but, I was free, single, unattached, unafraid, unengaged, and, untouched but, I was not un-affected. The men had come because of one reason, ME. The second week I was in Toronto my sister called me from Dominica to inform me that the American Embassy in Barbados had called to say that my American Visa was ready. I called the embassy and stated that I had now immigrated to Canada, and I asked that they forwarded the visa to my Canadian address. Within two weeks, I received the visa.

IT was the middle of May almost summer schools would soon be closing for summer vacation. I had doubts as to whether I could get a teaching position at that time; so I decided that I was not going to sit around and spend the meager bit of money I had come with to Canada. I went to the Canadian Bureau of Employment to seek for a job. They directed me to a kindergarten in a quiet part of the city, after interviewing me the owner gave me a favorable response and I was hired starting immediately. All went well for the week, but, on Friday morning, of the same week, a white young lady was hired. That very Friday afternoon, the owner handed me my pay for the week and she said "Never mind coming back, you cannot do the work"

On Monday I answered an advertisement posted on the outside door of an exclusive woman's dress shop in Willowdale, a suburb of Toronto, where the gentleman from Norton had taken me to visit his friends. I had noticed the big advertisement, a placard erected on the door the week before. The poster was still there, the job was still available. The owner interviewed me, she was impressed and she offered me the job that Monday. She inquired whether I could have started right away which I did. On Friday morning, that same week, a white girl was hired, that afternoon the lady paid me and said that my services were no longer required. Thus it was, two weeks in Canada, two different jobs, two times hired, two white girls hired, and I two times fired. I am black, and much more educated. I have had years of experience in working as a teacher and as a part time employee at a large department store where I performed various duties including sales and service in the ladies department. The following week, I was in contact with a former classmate who had immigrated to Canada on the Domestic Scheme a few years before, she informed me that the lady she worked for was seeking someone to work for her. This was of course a "live-in" job and I decided that I would try it at least through the summer in order to gather a few dollars rather than deplete the meager amount which I brought with me from Dominica. I seized the opportunity. My friend, having been in Canada for a number of years, she moved on with her education, she had a small apartment, and it appeared that she was working at an office, but she kept some sort of affiliation with her sponsor, now she wanted out of that situation. She arranged that I should come to speak with the lady at a time when she, my girlfriend was available. Well what do you know? I was totally taken by shock, I was horrified by the information which my friend was giving about me, all things made up portraying me as a very, destitute, lonesome friend who urgently needed somewhere to live and who she was eager to assist because I was poverty stricken and desolate. I was really dumb struck, shocked and stuck, but I needed a job. My living quarters would be a huge, open, not as quite warm basement playroom full of toys. The gentleman from Norton was visiting. I took him to witness my living space, the man was so appalled that he asked me to get my bag and go with him. I did not think that I should go. "You cannot live in such conditions" he pleaded, but I wasn't about to go to his hotel room. I did not. The gentleman from Norton called his friends in Willowdale related the situation to them and asked them whether they would have me stay with them for a while. They agreed and he drove me to the home of his friends. I soon took up work with another lady and things were not too bad apart from the fact that I was not really at ease doing this kind of work for a woman who was much younger than me watching over my shoulder much too often. There was a kind of condescending, not trusting way about her. Once I was in the toilet and she went around looking for me, she seemed a bit upset that I was not at her fingers' reach, she inquired as to where I was. I asked her whether I had to seek her permission to use the toilet. I wanted better, more freedom than this, after two weeks, another girlfriend informed me of a good family she worked with who wanted someone else, nice, to help with the chores. I applied and I was recruited. Working with this family was as good as one could expect or hope for. You were treated kindly and respectfully and since both of us were from Dominica and we knew each before, and the merit, justice, and wisdom, that, we had separate comfortable rooms made the situation very, pleasant, indeed. However, it was not my plan to remain a domestic maid. I applied to St. Michael Hospital in Toronto and got a job as a nursing assistant. I had always liked nursing, and I had come close to giving up teaching for nursing in Dominica. I worked as diligently as I could the staff was very cordial, and patients were very appreciative. I repaid the Canadian government for the loan which I had received to travel to Canada. I was free from obligation.

SEEKING LOVE

The gentleman from Norton visited again. He suggested that I should come to Massachusetts before too long. After three months working at St. Michael's Hospital, I tendered my resignation. The hospital staff told me they were sorry to see me go and informed me that if ever I wanted to return that they would be very happy to have me come. The unworthy and subtle, ugly prejudices I experienced, being fired from two jobs in two weeks only to be replaced by two less capable, less educated white girls, and driving around Toronto searching for advertised apartments, only to be told once your black face appeared that the apartments were taken. Once, I was informed that an apartment was available for rent. I tried to get it but was told that it was taken. I asked the gentleman from Norton to call the landlord, the apartment was still available. He asked to view the apartment and an appointment was arranged. The apartment was still available. The reality of it. The Gentleman from Norton could hardly believe the experience. Those were days of sharp awakening for him and much more also for me. I set my departure date to the U.S.A for October 31, 1967; five and one half months after I arrived in Canada, with the hope of seeking freedom and not be controlled by subtle racial prejudices: to observe, to learn, to find, and to experience, to examine, to decide and to know what love is, and most especially, and seriously, to choose one love from two Massachusetts men.

I knew the whereabouts of no one in the USA apart from the Gentleman from Norton and Augustus, since the Gentleman was older and he had never disrespected me, I thought it would be wiser to go to his home rather than at that of Augustus and that's how it was.

The gentleman from Norton had gotten me employment at Country Haven Nursing Home in Sharon, Massachusetts which was about fifteen to twenty miles from Norton; after a week of relaxation, I started work. The gentleman would take me to work every morning and pick me up every afternoon, never did I have to wait for him to come he was always waiting when I walked out the door. One day when I walked out the ground was covered beneath a blanket of cold, soft, white stuff, The Gentleman from Norton was overly excited to introduce me to it, he was like a father teaching his little daughter how to roll the magic white powder into small balls and pitch them away and how to form them into white bodies. It was a thrilling new experience, my first experience with snow.

Nine

LIVING IN THE USA, A LOVE TRIANGLE

Now that I was in Massachusetts I was anxious to meet Augustus, and really get to know him. I had made it known to both men that I was going to take my time to decide, neither of them pushed me, and that is exactly how I wanted it. Not expecting the unexpected can breed great expectations, glorious results. The gentleman from Norton offered to take me to Dorchester whenever I wanted to go. Though I could go by train, he volunteered to drive me, and he said to me "whenever you are ready to return give me a call and I will come and get you. Two is company three is a crowd. I was in the middle of a crowd. Two men both who had fallen in love with me and would trust me one to the other whom he knew was also in love with me. It was a very trying love triangle, but I was determined, sincere, and honest. I had to make a decision, and turn the tide. The more the gentleman from Norton drove me to Dorchester to the home of Augustus, the more my confidence in him grew, he was fifty-six, I was twenty-seven, he was Seventh Day Adventist, I was Catholic. He was white, I am negro. He was divorced and had two grown married daughters, one older, one younger than me. He had two granddaughters and two grandsons. I was single, never been married, free, disengaged, and a virgin woman. The Gentleman from Norton told me that he loved me deeply and that he wanted me very much. In reply I asked him "How would you like to have a child as dark as I am?" The man placed his beautiful blue eyes straight onto my dark brown eyes and without hesitating, with great assurance and without the shadow of a doubt, instantly replied, "I love you, don't I?"—That—struck a formidable note; because I already knew that he did. You may have realized that the gentleman from Norton was often on my mind, however, I was single, and disengaged. I moved to Dorchester to room with an old friend. It would be easier for me to asses Augustus, who was the same age as me, and like me, he was Catholic, he was negro, he had never been married, and he had no children. I had a phenomenal problem to solve, a serious matter to accomplish, an entangled love triangle to disentangle. I found employment at Lemuel Shattuck Hospital in Boston, while working there, I applied to nursing school. I realized quickly that not having attended high school, I had no education in Physics, Chemistry or Biology. I applied to Northeastern University in Boston and enrolled in the College of Education, I soon realized I was only repeating everything I had already studied as a teacher in Dominica. I transferred to the College of Business Administration to concentrate for a Major in Marketing, a Minor in Communication. Living in Dorchester, provided me the ease, the freedom, the time, the nearness, the contact, the perfect measurement tools for solving my love triangle. I was not getting sufficient food for my thoughts where Augustus was concerned. He simply was not growing up to my expectations. In the meantime, the gentleman from Norton visited me often, always inquiring, always planning, always hoping, never pushing, and I had become very aware that if I could not go somewhere whenever I had to work weekends, that he would not go either, even if he were invited. I was really falling in love with him, and I thought I would like to bear a child of this calibre of a man. My relationship with Augustus was on the decline. After years of correspondence, my interest in Augustus was ebbing away. As a matter of fact, I had long, since he lived in England, felt that he was not embracing the opportunities at his disposal for progress; he was not making himself available for growth and personal development. It now appeared to me that he was stagnant, and lacked motivation for his personal growth and self enrichment. Up until now I had preserved my Virginity for the man I should marry. The man who I decided really loved me; the one whose qualities I admired. The one I felt I really loved. I had given Augustus sufficient time and where with all to prove himself. Deep inside of me, I felt, I realized, I knew the gentleman from Norton loved me, and I him. I was ready to decide and move forward. One weekend I was visiting the gentleman in Norton and on May11, 1969, the die was cast. At the time I was attending a three month live in orientation program at Northeastern University I realized I missed my monthly period. I had no doubt that it was the work of May Day. I was really happy about the state of affairs for there were times when I wondered whether the gentleman was still capable of fathering children. I related my predicament to him he was happy and jubilant.

FOR MY BROTHER, MY SON

The gentleman from Norton asked that I moved to Norton after the Summer Orientation, which I did. He had one, his only living sibling, a sister two years younger. She was married and had one son, one daughter. They all enjoyed a good relationship. Her daughter was married and had also one son, one daughter. The gentleman from Norton related to me sometime that he mentioned to his sister that he was going to marry me to which she responded, "Don't marry her just keep her as a girlfriend." I felt betrayed for I thought we got along quite well, but, however she felt or whatever she meant, I knew that the man loved me very dearly and the decision to marry or not marry was not hers to make, neither did we need her permission nor her approval. He also mentioned that his only niece, his sister's daughter, that he had been very good to her, and that they were very close, and now, she too, was raising objections as to his relationship with me, and his wanting to marry me and he informed her to mind her own-business, and as a result their fondness of each other was growing cold and distant.

Because I had no family or relatives in the USA, The Gentleman From Norton and I went to Dominica to be married, but the fact that he was a divorcee, the Catholic Church would not allow us to marry in the Church. I stayed with my family for a few days then we returned to Norton and made other marriage arrangements. On October 11, 1969 We were married privately with Walter's sister and her husband, three friends from Dominica resident in the USA, one friend from Northeastern University, and a husband and wife who were friends of the Gentleman and also friends of his sister and her husband in attendance, at a multi-denominational church in Ridge, New Hampshire. We were now MR. and MRS. Walter Ellsworth Moorhouse. We then went for breakfast \brunch at a hotel cafeteria. Our guests departed and we drove happily through some wood lands towards Norton, Massachusetts.

I was a freshman at Northeastern University in Boston, some thirty eight to forty miles away from Norton. Walter drove me to Mansfield where I took a train most of the time and he picked me up almost right on time, every day. Whenever he could spare the extra time he would drive me to Northeastern. In the mornings he always prepared breakfast and fixed my carry-with me lunch, which I always enjoyed. He often had surprises therein. He was a good cook and he enjoyed cooking. Sometimes when I would be running late in the mornings, I would try to skip breakfast and, he would say, "After you have breakfast I will start the car." I never missed a class or a day from school, until February 18, 1970, we were in the midst of final examinations, Walter was driving me to Boston, I was catching up on some study, revising some notes. We were close to Northeastern

University when, all of a sudden, I felt severe pains in my stomach and I vomited. Walter drove me straight to Beth Israel Hospital, where we had arranged to have the baby. After examining me, the hospital staff told us that I was not ready, and therefore we should go home and return when the contractions were five minutes apart. We returned home and as we arrived inside, the contractions came very frequently and we headed for the hospital again. The baby was born at 2.55 pm that day. Walter would have liked and we had decided that should the baby be a boy we named the infant boy John William after Walter's only brother whom he said was a genius, whom he idolized, but who was drowned in a neighborhood swimming hole when the brother was ten years old, thus our baby boy was named John William; John William Moorhouse. Walter had informed me that he had two boys from his first marriage. They both died soon after their birth. I had discussed with Walter that I wanted to breast-feed the baby, he was not interested because at that time Americans seldom, if ever, breast-fed their babies, but I knew the benefits, I started breast feeding John in the hospital. When we got home, Walter would sit beside me at each feeding time and gaze in complete amazement, you could see he was enjoying the experience; he gazed with such intensity as though he was swallowing each gulp that John was pulling. Walter was extremely excited and interesting in every aspect of John's life, however, man can be jealous, and young mothers spend so much time staring over a new born baby checking to see that he is and keeps breathing, caring and loving their new born babies that too often they tend to forget and ignorantly pay scarce attention to their spouses. One night I was in John's room and I had just made myself comfortable on a bed in the nursery; Walter left his bed, came, took me by the hand, walked me to our bedroom while he said, "he will keep" I realized that Walter was feeling the pains of neglect and abandonment.

I had previously arranged for a leave of absence from school, so after John was born I stayed home with him. I read to him, sang to him, talked to him, rocked, him and played with him every single day, I read to him every night till he fell asleep. In the daytime, after my chores were done, as he grew older, I would pack a picnic basket, books, toys, crayons, and a blanket, and John and I we would picnic outside somewhere on home ground beneath the trees. He loved it and we had a marvelous time. I did this almost all the time.

When John was four months old I took him to the Caribbean so my folks would know him. I took him first to Aruba to meet with my very beloved Aunt Eunice, we then went to Barbados so my father who was an agriculturist there could see him, and then we went to Dominica to meet my mother, grandmother and oldest and youngest sisters. My two other sisters had immigrated to England. While we were in Dominica, at four-and-a-half months old, John took his first walk steps. He never crept, nor crawled. I could hardly believe my eyes. He was just a big live doll to everyone family and friends and children, especially children. From Dominica we went back home to Norton to a proud father anxiously awaiting his son's return and wanting anxiously to see him walk a few steps. Walter had two sons from his first marriage, both of whom died shortly after their birth. John was his new lease on life.

Our baby was doing very well and I continued to read to him regularly, you could see that he enjoyed the moments he listened attentively, and turned the pages to watch the pictures. He was a very happy baby, and he never got ill. When John was two years old he lost interest in eating and, since we were vegetarians, I thought that maybe he was lacking in nutrients. I took him to the doctor and requested a complete examination, the doctor after examining him thoroughly, informed me "Mrs. Moorhouse, John is perfectly healthy, he will eat when he is ready". One could have thought that the doctor was a prophet, the following week John started eating like before. We continued down the reading road, and, when he was three years old, one day we were sitting at the dining table and I was reading to him, John, he took the book from my hands and he said to me, "mummy I can read this" and he started to read. I was very amazed. I got some other books, he read all of them I was extremely delighted. Walter was enthusiastic. I decided that it was time therefore for me to return to Northeastern University. I re-enrolled, and when John was four years old, I went back to Northeastern taking John along with me. At this point in time, day care centers were not common, and I really did not cherish the idea of baby-sitters, so I packed John's bag with reading and coloring books, crayons, toys, snacks, clothes and a blanket, and we were of every day. It was an experience in itself both for him and for me, John was handsome, tidy, beautifully dressed, quiet, very interested and absorbed in his books, good mannered and well behaved. He disturbed no one, the students raved over him and the professors never, did one ever object. When I went to have my picture taken for my new identification card, the photographer smiled and talked with John; he took two pictures of John and made him a "'special' A mock ID '"everyone was so kind and understanding.

On the Mansfield train to and from Boston, John read everything in sight, and passengers stared in amazement and disbelief, a few times people congratulated him and gave him money.

When John was about seven years old, he came home one day and reported to me that some of his friends were trying to influence him to take some kind of a drug. I informed him that he had done a very clever thing in telling me about it and I instructed him about the dangers of using anything that people might try to force on him. Around that same time, I noticed that he was not performing as well as he could in mathematics, his father and I discussed the issues and we decided to take him to Dominica and put him in school there for a while. Kenneth was about six months old. I took the two boys to Dominica and enrolled John at the Seventh Day Elementary School in Roseau. John had lots of friends, he enjoyed being in Dominica and his Arithmetic improved steadily. We remained in Dominica for two school terms and returned to Norton for the next school year. John developed a love for mathematics and he did very well.

Two days after we were back in Norton, in August 1979 Hurricane David struck Dominica, that hurricane turned out to be the most disastrous hurricane to ever have struck the island. It caused tremendous devastation on the island the like of which we had not experienced before or witnessed since. Houses were destroyed, those standing were roofless. The two houses in which we were living were badly damaged, almost destroyed. But our folks were safe and well. One larger structure was built as replacement for the two small buildings. I returned to Dominica in

October two months after to assess the situation and assist my folks. I was much surprised to find that Dominica was like a ghost town, even the grass in the fields had all disappeared, the green slopes and hillsides turned to red earth and appeared lifeless, and trees standing naked were apparent everywhere and Dominica looked like a war zone with naked trees and some bare trunks shooting upwards in the air. It took longer than usual for trees to grow back, but Dominica is a very fertile place and the mountains are lush, the valleys are clean, the rivers clear and flowing and Dominica again displays its many shades of green and lush vegetation all across the island. It is amazing to visualize the new Dominica and rejoice in the real power and command of nature. It builds and it destroys, it creates things new like a new lake which formed in Dominica about ten years ago after an earthquake in the Layou valley area. "Miracle Lake" it is appropriately named; for it is indeed a miracle to have a new lake formed where no lake existed before. I had the unique and special experience to have had a pilot ex-boyfriend fly me over Miracle Lake in his private plane which he assembled himself; affording me that special double ecstasy, the joy, pleasure and delight of experiencing the grandeur and beauty of a new awe inspiring lake from up in the air and, in a home built, private custom plane. Experiences like that just cannot be duplicated and they live always as one's most memorable and interesting moments in life.

When I first enrolled at Northeastern, I was in the class of 1974. When I re-enrolled I was in the class of 1977. It seemed like I was a freshman again, my friends who had kept a Baby Shower for me in the school cafeteria had all graduated, I was now in a new arena with new players, new competitors, but, my study skills were much improved and I concentrated more on my work. My Marketing instructor was the chairman of the Marketing Department, Professor Duffton. In the senior year once he assigned the class to write a paper to develop a market strategy for introducing a new product which was soon to hit the market, when he had corrected the assignments, Professor Duffton came to class steaming and furious, stating that students had done very poorly, and that in the entire class of forty men and six women students there was only one "A." He cautioned students that they should take the assignments seriously since they were going to be the managers and executives of the future. He really laid it out on us in determined exuberant style. Everyone was ashamed and could hide for cover. When the papers were handed out, I peeped sheepishly at a corner of my paper, and, right on the top I observed "A+ Excellent!" Printed in red ink, I beamed with a sense of satisfaction, pride and accomplishment. Before my graduation, I sought some guidance and advice from Professor Duffton as to which career course he thought I should follow. He was very direct. "Mrs. Moorhouse, with your intelligence and ability, you should become a lawyer." I mentioned that I was amazed that he should say that since people had always been saying so to me when I was growing up in Dominica, but I had no interest in defending criminals. "You do not have to be a Criminal Lawyer" he asserted, "You could be a Civil Lawyer, a Real Estate Lawyer, a Business Lawyer, anything. I contemplated on the Professor's advice for a while and later I applied to Northeastern University Law School with Business Law in mind, meantime, my ability meanwhile had taken another direction, another baby boy was born on December 16,

1976, this one we named for me, 'Kenneth Jules' Kenneth Jules Moorhouse.

I had the good fortune of having to wait six months for students to finish their course requirements. In 1977 when Kenneth was six months old, I graduated and received a Bachelor of Science Degree in Marketing from the College of Business administration, Northeastern University Boston, Massachusetts. During my years at Northeastern University, I was very privileged to have worked on several co-operative work assignments, Research Assistant at Northeastern; Marketing Advertising Research at Texas Instruments, Attleboro; Assistant Manager Bridgewater State College Bookstore, and I was a substitute Teacher at Mansfield High School; all in Massachusetts. I also was very privileged to have my last six months at home, free to take care of Kenneth while I awaited members of my graduating class complete their course requirements for graduation. Like John, I breast fed Kenneth, this time, I didn't even give Kenneth water, only breast milk, and he developed beautifully. For the first ten months of Kenneth's life all he had was breast milk and you never saw a healthier, happier, well developed baby. He too, never got ill. We took him everywhere. I remember once we attended a court hearing of some important case which was being discussed in the courthouse, he was so quiet and well behaved. When Kenneth was two years old, I had a surprise a real surprise, another baby was on the way. Another boy was born on December 20, 1978. This one we named Walter Ellsworth, Walter Ellsworth Moorhouse JR. for his father.

I decided to stay home and raise my three boys, who were seven years, two years, and a newly born. I was twice pregnant and attending school all eighteen months of pregnancy with John and with Kenneth and never missed a day, thanks to the good, dear, living LORD. Now was the time to be mother and wife. I set my hopes of going to law school into the future.

My husband once remarked that because of my astuteness and forward manner perhaps I should seek employment. But, I am not the woman who values material accomplishments above the real true treasures and pleasures of nurturing children and working, or striving to inculcate moral values in them. I am mother, and there are no grandmother and aunties to help me. I have been raised to appreciate and hold on to the qualities which frame character and personality above material gain, at this point in time everything else was secondary. My children were first and foremost and I chose to be home with my boys where I felt I rightfully and truthfully belonged. Nothing else was as important to me. We could sacrifice, we could manage, and sacrifice and manage we did. The children would be the beneficiaries. The family would merit. As I look back I know that it has all paid off in great measures. All three of the boys have developed togetherness and closeness to each other, respect for their parents, and a simple, positive way of live devoid of greed, envy and jealousy, they are trustworthy, helpful to people and cooperate with each other.

They have never been prone to follow gangs but rather they depended on each other for direction, guidance and support which worked out beautifully. They never got into trouble but maintained the characteristics worthy of emulation and respect. They have very truly never caused me any worries which I relate back to my being home with them in their formative years. They have made me proud and I am indeed very happy, proud and appreciative of their personas.

I had a discussion with Walter regarding the sponsoring of my sisters to the USA. He thought that we should work at that project right away. We filed immigration papers on behalf of my four sisters, my oldest and the youngest lived in Dominica. They were eager and delighted about coming to the USA. The older and the younger sisters had immigrated to England they decided that they would remain in England. They both entered nursing school, and succeeded quite well. Sonia the older of the two studied midwifery, she became a nursing instructor. After forty years living in England Sonia went on a vacation to Dominica, she did not return to England, but rather she started a building project in Copt Hall which she personally supervised. She decided she was not returning to England. Her husband joined her a few years later and there in Copt Hall, in the lovely, beautiful Roseau Valley they remained and run what is their Roseau Valley hotel.

Sonia has made two trips to the USA, one to visit me in Florida, one to visit our two sisters in Boston.

Myrtle studied pediatric nursing and was a registered pediatric nurse. After her son was born she switched occupation and took a position with Cable and Wireless in order that she would have more time to raise her son. She visited Dominica a couple times, she visited us in the USA but she maintains residency in England.

THROW A LITTLE LIGHT ON THE DARK SUBJECT

Walter Sr. was a very accomplished machinist, the best you could find. He was self employed and worked from home. I imagine he must always have been a genius though he did not have a high school education. His was a one-man-shop situated in a section of the large basement of the sprawling sixteen room two and a half floor colonial house on eleven and one half acres which he purchased when he was just twenty three years of age. The kind of machinery that he owned, the magnitude of the objects he worked on, things including giant steel bow thruster shafts for ocean going ships, his attention to great detail, the high quality work that he delivered working on projects for Procter and Gamble the soap company, the Mansfield Chocolate company, and other suchlike companies. This man did the work that no other machinist could touch, never mind work upon. These certain companies sought him, and he sought and gained their work, but, like my mother, he wasn't paid his true worth, he was grossly underpaid and he barely edged out a living wage. He did everything himself. Someone who was as efficient and reliable in production and delivery of such quality work on time as he did, should never have his talent abused and robbed as he was dealt, but, I suppose that is the mortal sin of capitalism, one thrives at the mercy and goodness, or the ignorance or weakness and at the expense of others. Walter should have extended his business and employed even one assistant. I advised him to that direction but he lacked that confidence and financial capability, and he thought the magnitude and kind of work he did that he could not entrust it to anyone, so he did everything, cut everything, mold everything, shape everything, work on everything, market everything himself sell what you design, arrange everything, plan everything, go search for everything: but, he never earned everything. His earnings were much below his capabilities. The only thing he did not do himself was that he had someone else work on his accounts, the perfect example of honesty and integrity. Money was not in abundance, but Walter well knew what lay ahead. I really never realized nor understood the full depths and wisdom of it all. Only now, in all honesty, do I feel the wisdom of the man, his foresight in having a certified accountant, work on his financial transactions. He was a very practical, deep thinking, thoughtful, kind and generous honest man, with great foresight and tremendous fortitude, to whom and for which, I, my family, my children and family owe a great debt and honor. Our three sons received Social security benefits, till they turned eighteen, and as his widow I do receive social security payments on his work merits, since, thanks to his genius and the credible delivery system of the Federal government, who advises on fair output, input and intake, I would have been receiving less on my own merit, having been a stay at home mother longer than I had been a wage earner.

Walter loved to garden, every summer he grew all kinds of vegetables and lots and lots of corn, he canned all kinds of food and froze a whole deal more. We would travel to Boston every Saturday night to go to the Italian Market at closing time, where he got bushels of produce: onions, potatoes, celery, lettuce, Carrots, etc. etc. for a dollar a sack-full or so, sometimes when the vendors wanted to leave, he got produce for simply picking them up.

I remember one Saturday night we had the most frightening experience, we were shopping around, and at one point I was alone, I thought that John must have been with his dad, but I turned around anyway and walked in the opposition direction to join them. I spotted Walter quickly but John was not with him. I froze. "Where is John?" I asked him, "I thought he was with you" Walter replied, we were both dumbfounded and we looked around in earnest and mentioned to people that we were looking for a little boy about three years old who had strayed away from us. Luckily, we did not look for long and we found John beside a couple who said to us that they were wondering who the little boy was with. We felt guilty that our son must have agonized a while and we were thankful that we found him quickly safe and sound. We realized how easy it was for children to get dispersed from those who are responsible of attending to them, how easy it is for them to get lost in a crowd and separate from people in their control. The outcome could have been very different. We were indeed very fortunate, thankful and relieved to have him back with us in quick time.

Walter was a very practical person, and a great outdoors man also, we went mushroom hunting, and picking wild grapes, wild apples, and berries which he pressed into sauces and juices and preserved plenty of them. In the spring we collected water cress and went herring catching. This was a new and exciting educational experience for me. It was the fist time in my life that I was seeing fresh herrings, seeing them in their natural habitat swimming up and down in fresh clear flowing springs, millions of them so thick in the water, you could catch them with bare hands which I did for the fun, enjoyment and experience of it. People came with nets attached to long rods, and scooped herrings like one would scoop leaves from the yard after sweeping them into a pile, such amazing experiences. We caught bushels of herrings which Walter processed like canned sardines. Those were delicious and a big favorite of mine. Some of the herrings he used for fertilizer in his garden.

In Dominica herrings were an imported product. They were either in salted brine and kept in a huge wooden barrel or they were salted and smoked brown and dry.

Every summer we got blue fish and other fish from the fish piers. We froze a great deal and we distributed vegetables and fish to our neighbors and friends in Boston. Our basement was always filled with, various foods, drinks and sauces, well preserved for the fall and winter months. We had the very best for food but our cash expenditure on food was very minimal. Of course we purchased gasoline, and spent time to preserve the foods; but that was time made so much more precious than usual. People from our neighborhood and friends from Boston delighted to come and enjoy times with us. We always had good times.

Walter firmly believed that corn was at its best flavor and nutritional content and value when it was cooked right after it was picked. In the summer we had the best time of all, we would wait till the company arrived and then we would all go corn picking, then we husked the corn while the water was boiling and served it hot right from the fire. I had never eaten corn so fresh or tasted so good, or seen people eat so much corn or have such a great time. We enjoyed ourselves tremendously. We were having company one day, dinner was all ready, the table was set, folks were all seated, we awaited Walter, it was getting a bit dark, the lights were still off, and we were ready to start eating, Walter walked in from outside, I was the only dark skinned person present that day, "Throw A Little Light On The Dark Subject," my husband said, laughing as he turned on the lights; everyone roared with laughter, it was so spontaneous, and we settled down to dinner.

He may not have known it, and he never realized his true worth, but that man taught me so very much. He certainly threw a light upon this dark subject. He was a very practical man. The manner in which he provided the needs of his family, his helpfulness, generosity and kindness to other people, were his signature and very admirable. They were his virtual strength. His love of nature, adventure and the simple life were extremely remarkable.

Walter was very accustomed to deny himself of anything and give it to someone else. At the same notion he would not accept gifts from anyone as he thought he would be imposing on them. I tried to explain to him that the joy and satisfaction which he got from giving to others, some folks would love to experience that same feeling of having him accept something from them. He understood and I saw a reluctant small change. One day I arrived home and saw an empty spot with dirt still very freshly turned, I wondered what had happened, as I walked towards the door, I looked across the street and noticed a young red maple tree planted in the neighbor's yard. I knew very well that there was no red maple there before. I turned around to visit my red maple tree, these were very rare, and sure enough where my maple tree was growing, was now the empty parch. Some other time I arrived just in time to find a husband and wife friend of my husband loading into a container, in the trunk of their pickup truck, a beautiful baby-rose bush we had growing. This time I raised my objection and I had the couple leave without the baby-rose bush.

This man, Walter, would dig his heart out and give to anyone who wanted it, his friends all knew it and many of them imposed on his good nature. He performed that sort of behavior over and over again. I do know I missed some of my most cherished possessions, my silver USA coins, a special hand knitted baby blanket, my '"A+ excellent "only *****A*****in class,-college paper"' gold trimmed clear kitchen ware etc, leave me wondering. But, be what may, no one of us is without flaw, no one is perfect. We all are subject to mistakes of one kind or another. We should attempt to be forgiving. Walter was, good to me, in several masterful and endearing, rich and powerful ways. He had been always proud and delighted in taking me anywhere. He took me everywhere, Boston Symphony, Brockton Symphony, Rhode Island Sound, Martha's Vineyard, Woods Hole, Nantucket Island Sound, Fisherman's Wharf, New Hampshire, Vermont, Maine, Sandwich Beach, Durgin Park the oldest restaurant in the country, and restaurants everywhere. Once, when our three sons were still quite small, Walter took the family to a popular restaurant on Cape Cod somewhere I don't remember exactly where. There was a very long line waiting all through to outside and we waited for quite sometime. Our three little boys were as well behaved and orderly as any parent would want them to be, they were well dressed and handsome. When our turn arrived, Walter approached the counter and placed his order, as he pulled out his wallet, the cashier said to him. "Sir, your bill for your entire family has already been paid for by someone who wants you to know that the boys are so very well behaved and attractive that he is delighted and pleased to pick up the tab on their behalf. "We were very delighted and we re-enforced the significance and benefits of good behavior right then and there to our beloved, well mannered sons.

To Florida the family went for Christmas when John was four years old, and, then to England for New Year, John and I, to visit my older and younger sisters those two who John had not met in Dominica. Walter had often heard me say that I had not seen my sisters in years. "get your things ready" he told me," one day after we returned home from Florida. "I am sending you to England to visit your sisters whom you keep crying about". He could not have done anything better. It was a real treat. I was overly excited that I would be seeing my sisters after fourteen years of separation. They had wondered whether they would recognize me when they came to meet me at the airport but they reported they had no difficulty as they found that I resembled our mother quite so much. We roamed over Old London Town we visited museums, the automobile museum, Madam Tussaud's and name sake towns and places. Many towns in

New England, New England itself are named after towns in England: Sharon, Taunton, Cambridge, Bridgewater, Mansfield, etc. when we got to Norton, England, we visited the Norton Brewery. The folks there were so excited to find out that we were from Norton, Massachusetts U S A. They presented us with a big bottle of champagne.

One day, Walter came home hurrying to me, "get dressed," he said "I want to show you something" he took me on a forty mile drive to show me a dress which he liked that he saw on display in a store window which he wanted me to have. He was not accustomed to buying me clothes, I should be happy about this attempt, but, one misses out sometimes for lack of perception and I made the biggest mistake, I told him I did not like the black top, red bodied, black belted dress. I shattered the man's pride and devastated his enthusiasm. He swore he would never buy me anything again. BUT, he bought me a lovely hair dryer for my birthday soon after. When I saw the beautiful, salon styled hair drying handbag looking machine, I saw my sister Beatrice, who was doing hair dressing on coal pot and hot iron in Dominica without the convenience of hair dryers, they washed the hair at home in the morning and let it dry out throughout the day for an afternoon after work hair session. I knew a hair dryer would ease her work and increase her income potential enormously. A few days after I received the precious, useful, smiling, enticing, hair dryer, I hid it away in my closet. Within a few weeks I mailed the traveling hair dryer to Dominica. Walter never dreamed the course or the tale of the economic hair dryer, except that he had bought one for me. Maybe he didn't even remember that.

Before I knew him, Walter had had a terrible accident in his workshop, a huge and extremely heavy metal cylinder had fallen on his leg and crashed it. By the time he got to hospital, plus waiting to be attended; it was too late; too demolished, too damaged for repair; gangrene had taken over, his leg had to be amputated. He therefore wore an artificial leg, and lucky enough for him the leg was hardly noticeable to anyone. After we married I noticed that he would accompany his sister and I to the beach but he would never undress, never mind getting in the water. One day I had a discussion with him, I explained that his circumstances are what they are and since he was never going to grow a new leg he should therefore accept his predicament, move forward and stop robbing himself of the enjoyment of swimming, that he should accustom himself to the situation and brave himself, even if people would stare at him for a while the satisfaction he would have for overcoming that fear and partaking in the joy of swimming would create much happiness for him. He must have realized the merit of my admonition. I was indeed gratified that soon, the impossible became a reality as Walter hopped one arm around my shoulders, my arm around his waist off to the shore and going swimming. I was pleasantly surprised and full of gladness and satisfaction to discover how happy that made him and to find that he was really an avid very prolific swimmer and he had found the renewed joy and pleasure of swimming, which he did frequently henceforth. The irony remains that to this day I am not a swimmer, but the joy and satisfaction I had of watching him swim and enjoying himself again, especially when in later years, he led our three little boys to the water that was joy way beyond compare. This is a man who really enjoyed outdoor life; swimming naturally became a frequent item on his agenda and not only would he go swimming, but he would chose the most pleasant areas he knew of and take the family to swimming holes and places he knew so well and once enjoyed; places near, and places not so near, the family went swimming. This brings to my mind a time before the children were born, he and I were out driving around the country, we came to a lovely abandoned estate with a clean clear flowing stream projecting a small waterfall. We did not have swimming clothes with us that day for we had not planned on swimming. The environment was so peaceful, private and serene, so enticing I decided to take a dip and enjoy the luxury afforded us for a moment. Before long I was in the water, bare bodied. The water was very refreshing and I was having a great relaxing time enjoying a bit of freedom. Walter did not come in. I splashed and splashed around and was having a good time remembering the times I had like this in Dominica; and my goodness, as I turned around ready to join Walter, there he was in the company of two other men about his age who were also enjoying the countryside. They were all laughing as they looked in my direction. You would have thought that Walter would have alerted me, but no, why should he spoil the fun that they were all having, three senior white men watching a black naked, young woman splashing in a clear running stream off a quiet country dirt road. I bet it was the first time they had experienced something like this, why would they not enjoy their moment. Scenes like that would seldom if ever come their way again. As far as Walter was concerned it must have been the more, the merrier. More surprise, more people to stare, more fun, more excitement.

Years later, we were in Dominica, all fears of staring eyes at his amputated leg removed, we were having a picnic on the rough eastern coast of Dominica, on the Atlantic shore; Walter joined local folks in the water, but stubborn, as he could be, he paid little attention to warnings, that he should be watchful of the ebbing tides. Walter desired to go for a swim, when he decided to come ashore, the tide and easing flow of sand said no, not so fast. As he struggled to make for the shore, and almost there, he was dragged in, he tried to come but experienced difficulty, he tried again, his one leg lifted up to the sky, he was of course on his back as we quickly grabbed his shoulders and dragged him out to safer ground.

He must have felt relieved and appreciative that the folks got him in time. It was a scary moment, and no teasing matter.

Twelve

MOORE PARK

Walter received a letter from an English couple resident in Dominica whom he had met on his trips there, the letter relating that they were selling their property and they were affording him first choice before placing the property on the market. Walter and the couple had all been interested in purchasing that certain property in Moore Park, eleven years earlier; being resident on the island, the couple had the opportunity to negotiate directly and they bought the property. They were a retired English couple, and they loved the place very much, but in 1979 Hurricane David devastated the island, telephone lines were destroyed, roads were in an upheaval, traveling was difficult. Their only son visited them he did not want to reside in Dominica. The folks wanted to sell everything. They had previously informed Walter, but he thought their price was too high. They were now informing him that they decided to lower the price from that which they had quoted him earlier. Walter was excited. "If you really are interested, I think that you should go very soon and that you should take a deposit with you". I said to him "If I go I want you to come with me" he replied, we arranged with a family friend to take care of the children and we were gone in a few days. The timing of this whole matter could not have been better. It was a matter arranged and decided in Heaven. Walter loves living quietly away from the hustle and bustle of the city, the government had recently acquired a portion of his Norton property for the construction of a new interstate, highway, he wanted no part of this property anymore, he hated the thoughts of a busy highway in his backyard, he wanted OUT. He had grown to love Dominica and thought it was Paradise, and he wished to reside there. THIS WAS HIS MOMENT.

Walter had often spoken of his desire to own forty to-sixty acres in the middle of the forest somewhere in Dominica. Thoughts of living in the middle of a forest in the wilderness away from other folks did not set well with me. I had never been to Moore Park before. The day we arrived I thought that it seemed the perfect place, set as it were on forty seven and one half acres at the top of a hill half a mile away from the village proper with the driveway well off the road and the village a picturesque sight further down in the valley below affording beautiful, gorgeous scenes all the way and views of The Atlantic Ocean gleaming in the distance from the front porch. The four of us settled quickly into business discussing price and other things pertinent to the estate, after a little while I walked outside, to the back porch, and, just as I wished, the lady followed. We had our own discussions and I seized the opportunity. "If you would decrease the price, we would give you a down payment right now." I said to her, she stared at me for a moment in complete amazement almost as though she could not believe her ears; in a second, she rushed inside and spoke with her husband. The deal was struck. The four of us discussed some more, and Walter wrote them a check Thus It was the first day I ever stepped on Moore Park Estate; we became the owners. We were very proud of what we had accomplished. We arranged when we would return to claim full ownership. The lady, Mrs. Stock decided on February 16, 1981.

We spent a few days with my folks in Roseau, and we were back in Norton. Walter's dream had come true, but he could not come to Dominica right away, he was the sole breadwinner, and since he was no longer interested in the Norton property, he wished to sell it, all of it, he therefore had to get the property on the market and he wanted everything sold before he left, the house, the shop, the equipment, everything. He simply wanted no part of that property anymore. He was anxious to retire to Dominica.

In the meantime my sisters received their visas for permanent residence in the USA. They were anxious to come. It is coincidental that we would have to cross paths, but we had arranged to be in Dominica for February 16, 1981. Mr. and Mrs. Stock had set the date and they had arranged their departure. We were determined to keep our appointment. WE decided my sisters and their families would reside with my husband and oldest son while I and my youngest two sons would go to Dominica. We all managed well, my sisters were home in Norton with Walter and John for six months. They learned their way around quickly. The four adults all found employment. They all moved to Boston to learn, to discover, to observe, to work, and to participate, in life in the USA, and to endeavor and strive to achieve the American Dream.

John was very impressed with the relationships between my sisters and me, and the closeness and bond between us, one day he remarked, "Mummy you and your sisters are so close to each other you get along so well, and you help and look out for each other. I hope that when we grow up we will be as close to each other as you all are." "You have to work at it my dear, feel and show love for each other, you have to care for each other and help each other and you will be happy for it."

My oldest sister worked in a nursing home. Her husband joined her in Boston. He too found employment. Together, they saved and saved, and saved till they saved enough to afford the down payment on a home in Brockton MA. Her son worked at a courthouse for a while. He then enrolled in The American Service where he is now a sergeant.

My youngest sister, after working for a while, she went to college and obtained her bachelor's degree. She then began working on her Master's degree while working on a fulltime job at a hospital she obtained her Master's Degree. She is now Superintendent of a Head Start program in a Boston ABCD☹ (Action for Boston Community Development) where she trains young minds and staff. Her husband followed, he went to college and obtained his Bachelor's and his Master's Degree. He is now the CEO at the Brockton YMCA. They too purchased their home. Two of their three children went to college, married and purchased their homes. The third is self employed and runs a Barber Shop in Boston.

In our discussions I mentioned to Walter that I did not think it was sensible to sell everything since he had no idea how he would adjust to living in Dominica and that he might want to return, so he should at least retain a portion of the land. In his determination to confirm that he wanted completely out of there, he said to me, "If you want this place in Dominica you have to go and take care of it." I thought this possibility over and over and over again, there I was about to enter Law School, but, my husband wants me to go to Dominica; *I reasoned and thought to myself, people go to school to acquire a good education, to earn big money, to buy what they want, if my husband is now buying me a beautiful property in my homeland, I had better seize the opportunity*. Thus, Walter threw the light upon this dark subject once more.

On February 16, 1981 Walter Jr. two-and-one half years old, and I arrived in Moore Park. We spent one week with the Stocks while they introduced us to persons and offices that were important in the exchange of ownership and the proceedings of running the agricultural estate. The following week the folks were gone, back to England, I was again resident in Dominica and the proud owner of Moore Park Estate.

I was a stranger in the place since I had visited there only once before, the day we purchased the property, but, I was very excited, eager and determined to get everything under control. Four months later, I left a trusted friend to hold the fort. I returned to Norton to visit the family but more especially and purposefully, to take Kenneth, now four-and-one-half years old, to Dominica. We decided that John, who was eleven years old, would remain with daddy to allow him to graduate from Middle School. I was back to DOMINICA and we were living in two separate worlds of two very different cultures, my husband's, the American, and mine, a Dominican West Indian.

Walter experienced some difficulty in finding a suitable buyer for the Norton property, since he wanted to sell everything, house and shop to one buyer, He persevered, and he eventually persuaded a friend of his, a builder who purchased the property lock, stock, and barrel.

Walter had really grown to think that Dominica was a paradise, the best place for peace and tranquility, and he was especially serious about raising his sons there away from the complexes of a big metropolis. He was anxious to go.

John graduated, from Norton Middle School, Kenny and Walter JR. Were not yet of school age, I was home maker, mother, and farmer. The coast was clear. Walter was determined that he was not going to remain in Norton another winter, he asked me to come to choose the items which I intended to keep, I returned to Norton, selected what I wanted, stayed two weeks and returned to Dominica. Walter had our belongings shipped to Dominica and in September 1983, with his oldest son, John, the Gentleman from Norton, Massachusetts who had filed immigration papers for me to reside in the USA where I became a naturalized American, he moved to Dominica, West Indies, the place where we met on his first visit there in1966, to join me and his youngest two sons eagerly awaiting his HOMECOMING, to establish permanent residence, to retire, begin a new life, and to enjoy the peace, quiet and unspoiled, rugged, natural beauty of Dominica, the place and its people he thought was Paradise, which he had grown to love so very much. He had grown to think that Dominica was the best place on earth, and he sincerely wanted to raise his sons there among gentle, peaceful loving people, to live a simple life away from the big cities. Walter, being self employed, he had not retired. He was now sixty-nine years old with three young sons, ages, thirteen, seven, and five whom he loved adoringly. I knew he had proven his love for me, now it was my turn to prove how sincerely I loved him. This was a turning point in the lives of each one of us, there I was, about to enter Business Law School, John having graduated from Norton Middle School he was set to enter high school, Kenneth was enrolled in elementary school in Paix Bouche, Dominica, Walter Jr. to begin elementary school and Walter Sr. to take up residence in a foreign country with a completely different culture.

It was my privilege and honor to have this opportunity to raise my sons in the environment where I was born, one of simplicity, with a year round summer climate, a place where material things were secondary to friendliness, caring, and sharing, a place where rules of etiquette and respect ruled supreme values I do esteem so very highly. It was gratifying that I could play a part to help my husband to retire happily. THIS WAS HIS MOMENT.

Life in Dominica would be very different for him, everything from fish to bread, from having many good old friends to making completely new friends. Though people move around and change residence often and again, these events are sure to have repercussions on a sixty nine year old man.

However Walter was a man with an amazingly friendly and helpful attitude, there was no doubt that he would be indoctrinated into the Dominican society with ease and in quick time so we cast all fears and uncertainty aside as we contemplated towards a bright, healthy and happy life in Dominica.

SCHOOL TIME: PRINCIPAL

I enrolled John at the Seventh Day Adventist Secondary School in Portsmouth, and Kenneth and Walter JR. at the Seventh Day Adventist Elementary School in Bense. Soon after, perhaps knowing that I was a college graduate and one with much experience in teaching and knowing well that all my three children were in Adventist Schools and that I was home not working out; news of the need for a school principal at the Bense Adventist Elementary School where my youngest two boys would be students; was circulating. I loved teaching and I had been a very well known capable, accomplished, experienced teacher, I was approached, I applied and got the post.

By the time Walter arrived, to reside in Dominica, I was school principal and marketing produce which I had planted on the estate, this was very gratifying, we had a great feeling of achievement, that we were already earning money from our investment, and now I was School Principal, we were enjoying some degree of upward mobility. The boys settled in well and had lots of friends, Walter Sr. was naturally a friendly person anyway, everybody loved him, and life was great. Soon his sister visited us from Mansfield, Massachusetts, this was her first trip to the Caribbean and we were determined to give her a wonderful time. We showed her around the island, took her to the most interesting sights, and introduced her to our friends.

Shortly after I became the principal of The Bense Seventh Day Adventist Elementary School ; the government announced that the president of Dominica would be visiting all the government run schools on the island, no mention was made of other schools, I thought this was an affront to all students who did not attend government schools, I wrote to the education department explaining that all students were citizens of the state and that it was unfair and unwise for the president to visit some schools and ignore those which were not government run, that all students as well as their parents were citizens of the state and they too needed as much, to know their president. Shortly thereafter, I received correspondence from the education department apologizing for their mishap and a rescheduled program for the president's itieniary which included the date and time when President Signoret would visit The Bense Seventh Day Adventist Elementary School. I was much gratified and I set to formulate a program of activities to welcome the president and his entourage. Everything went smoothly the students were diligent and poised, the teachers eager and cooperative. I was overwhelmed and was congratulated for my efforts. President Signoret and I became good acquaintances thereafter and he always recognized me wherever we were at the same forum.

Another of my favorite happenings while I was principal of the Bense Seventh Day Adventist School lies in the preparation of students to sit the Common Entrance Examinations to high school, when the results were published, the Bense Seventh Day Adventist Elementary School received its first ever qualifying grades. This was a real achievement for the school and one of which I was very proud indeed.

The boys were back in school, I kept busy on the estate planting crops and harvesting. I sold produce at the market and at the hotels in Portsmouth. I enjoyed this very much, as soon as the boys left for school I would go to the vegetable garden. I concentrated on crops which matured quickly, string beans was my favorite of all, parsley, thyme, celery, radish chive, these grew quickly so I could reap and sell quickly, it was a tremendous experience. On moonlight nights I would work on a special garden close to the kitchen which I had planted with the children in mind I determined that I was going to prepare menus and give them a diet based more on local than imported foods, green bananas and dasheen instead of rice or macaroni. Since they were not accustomed to the local produce, I had to prepare them in ways that they would enjoy, so I needed to have the products available. The people who were employed were responsible for planting and handling the bananas and other field crops. In Norton the children's father planted and preserved foods in summer for use in fall and winter. Dominica has a tropical climate you plant all year, harvest all year there was no need to preserve. Life was a dream, and we certainly enjoyed happy fulfilling times. I was filled with strong confidence that the children and I would do just fine. I focused attention and set our priorities on matters beneficial in achieving a happy and fruitful life.

Life is full of challenges, there are flaws in human nature and sometimes things do not work as they should, sometimes because of envy, sometimes because of jealousy, people act viciously. As school principal I received an invitation from the East Caribbean Conference of Seventh Day Adventists of which Dominica is a contributing member, inviting my husband and me to a conference for workers of the conference to be held in Barbados. I attended, my husband did not. Receiving the invitation and attending, seemed to have been too much, too good, too soon, as some people are eager to sabotage others and squeeze and victimize them. They are never to encourage, nor to emulate. Persons from the church I attended, those who were the leaders, those whom I encouraged and advised, those to whom I preached the benefits of a college education and how and where they could raise the funds to send their daughter to college,(she had been "the principal" without qualifications) they pulled the rug from under me. Dissatisfaction, gossip, slander, I was not a good teacher, I was this and that and the other; fabrications, false allegations and dispute quickly became a new mode of ethics and interaction; A New Deal in character deformation. Soon, perhaps too soon, I tendered my resignation from the Bense Adventist Elementary School so those who were eager for a position for their soon to graduate offspring they would have me in their way no more.

But I was in Dominica, and the Eastern Caribbean Conference was aware of my accomplishments, their assessment of my performance by a well renowned, very respected, senior pastor who had visited the school was very positive, he noticed the difference, the progress, they would not accept my resignation and wished that

I continued as principal. The cold war intensified, the young lady graduated from college, and the pressure grew more subtle, but intensely severe. I would not fight, I did not fight I did not have to fight. I did not need to fight. I re-submitted my resignation and I left the island for a vacation in the USA. Before long, the young lady was principal. Mission Accomplished! During that same time my husband was visiting the USA; word came that he was ill and hospitalized. He was a patient at a Rhode Island hospital, diagnosis, lung cancer. When I visited this tall, sturdy, medium built man who had never been ill, he had grown very slender in such a short space of time. I saw that his chances for recovery were not very positive. I mentioned that I would bring the children to visit. "NO" he replied quickly, vehemently, "let them remember me the way they knew me". With this information I returned to Dominica to inform the children's caretaker that I would be returning to the U.S immediately and without the children, the next day, the evening before my departure, the telephone rang, it was my step daughter conveying the message that her father had breathed his last. "Hold everything till I come," I said to her, the next morning I was on my way to West Virginia to my step daughter's home taking John with me.

Walter in his usual, unselfish, forward looking, anticipating self had previously discussed with me that funerals were too expensive and he would therefore prefer to be cremated, so whatever little he had would go towards raising the boys, rather than on a lavish funeral, and so it was.

I was unaccustomed to the rules of engagement for funerals in the USA. I invited no one, but his sister and daughter arranged a ceremony. I had determined to take my husband's ashes to Dominica and bury them in a valley on his place in the sun beneath and between the mountains which he loved so much but, after discussing this with my oldest sister, her advice was to the contrary, she thought it would be better and wiser if I buried him here in the U.S.A. since cremation was not practiced in Dominica, she thought the folks in Moore Park might think I was evil spirited. Walter's ashes were therefore interred beside his mother in Mansfield, Massachusetts; so in Mansfield he was born, in Mansfield he was left and in Mansfield he blends with the earth.

The boys were back in school, I kept busy on the estate planting crops and harvesting. I sold produce at the market and at the hotels in Portsmouth. I enjoyed this very much, as soon as the boys left for school in the mornings I would go to the vegetable garden. I concentrated on crops which matured quickly, string beans was my favorite of all, parsley, thyme, celery, radish chive, these grew quickly so I could reap and sell quickly, it was a tremendous experience. On moonlight nights I would work on a special garden close to the kitchen which I had planted with the children in mind, I determined that I was going to prepare menus and give them a diet based more on local than imported foods, green bananas and dasheen instead of rice or macaroni. Since they were not accustomed to the local produce, I had to prepare them in ways that they would enjoy, so I needed to have the products available. The people who were employed were responsible for planting and handling the bananas and other field crops.

Whereas in Massachusetts the children's father planted in summer and preserved food for use in fall and winter,

Dominica has a tropical climate, you can plant all year round, harvest all year round so there is no need to preserve any produce. Tree crops are different as most tree crops bear fruits once a year. But there again different fruits blossom and bear at different times of the year so there are always fruits of one kind or another available all year. We had most of what we needed; life was a dream, and we certainly enjoyed happy fulfilling times. As we became more accustomed to living on the farm, we adjusted and tried to make farm life more pleasant and profitable. We were out joyriding around the island one day and we came across a big Bedford truck with a "for sale" sign on it. We approached the owner to find the details and we decided to buy the truck. We did some repair work and the truck was ready for the road. We previously hired a truck owner to transport our bananas to the buying house; John could now transport our bananas himself, in addition he was hired by other farmers to transport their bananas to the buying and packing plant. He was thrilled with the outcome and he developed a strategy where he recruited other farmers. He formulated a time delivery system, He was very dependable and the farmers liked doing business with him, he was having a great experience and a good time. He determined to increase production on the farm, we employed more workers and our yield grew steadily. News reached the agriculture department of the terrific farm work John was doing and they came to observe and record his adventures. It is amazing how news gets around and how people register in their minds things that hold interest to them. About two years later I was vending tourist items at the vendors market. A woman from Trinidad and Tobago asked me a question when I replied she asked "are you the mother of the boys who were shown on television planting bananas?"

"yes I am" I replied, I was stunned and I asked her why she asked "I recognized the voice she said" so I wanted to know if that were you" I was really amazed a person who lived in Trinidad would have noticed, recognized my voice, and remembered so vividly.

Life takes its own directions and often things we do are determined and influenced by factors way beyond our own control but I was confident we would do just fine. I focused attention and set our priorities on matters beneficial to achieving to happy and fruitful life.

Meanwhile Mr. Lobelieus a man who had visited my husband several times before in connection with a portion of land which he claimed belonged to a client of his visited

He mentioned that the client had passed away and he wanted to clear the situation. He took the boys and I out to dinner and we developed a closer relationship. Mr. Lobelieus was interested in trying to get that piece of land which he claimed was affixed to our deed. Since he could not produce any documents to prove his claim I paid him little attention in that regard. He visited me again. Meantime we were doing a general cleaning and Kenneth found a stack of old maps. On one of those maps was a hand drawn line across a corner of the map. As one who does not want anything which does not rightly belong to her, whether he was right or not I told Mr. Lobelieus about the map. He stated that that was the portion of land to which he was referring. I mentioned that he proceed to clear the matter. He approached a lawyer and the plot of land was deeded to him. Now that my husband had passed away he visited often, we developed a closer relationship, got attracted to each other and fell in love.

We married shortly after. Mr. Lobelieus was my senior by a number of years. He was an Orthodox Catholic Bishop, and a trained accountant. I thought I was fortunate to have a good companion one who would assist me in raising the boys and be a mentor to them.

I was accustomed to buy our household products in wholesale allotments so we always had plenty of supplies. At one point our milk was running low, since I had planned to go to the city the next day I decided I would wait to get milk at the same time. Mr. Lobelieus wanted a cup of coffee he decided to walk to the village shop, he returned with a very small can of milk just enough for his coffee, this by the way was the first thing he brought to the home though he used milk and had his meals everyday. I stared at him in disgust as he drank his coffee and I wondered whether he was thinking right.

Two weeks later while cleaning there was a few magazines on Mr. Lobelieus' bedside table, I opened a magazine inside the magazine were two airline tickets, one for him, one for his daughter who was visiting her relatives in St. Joseph.

These inconsistencies led me to think that I had fallen victim to Lobelieus' malpractices and that his attraction was never based on love but on deceitful motives.

We were accustomed to attend church services on Saturdays, the first Saturday after I saw the airline tickets in the magazine, he told me that he was not going to church that day and asked that I let the boys stay home with him. I did not and I had the boys all go to church with me, when we returned home, Mr. Lobelieus with a few pieces of clothing and a small black umbrella belonging to him were all gone, no communication exchanged, no explanation given, no questions asked. He was gone. I felt relieved and I asked the boys to get on their knees and we thanked God.

Shortly afterwards I went to the US on business when I called home, the children's caretaker related to me that Mr. Lobelieus had called to say that he was attacked and robbed off his money while on his way to Sweden and he had called to ask if I could come and help him. He had the audacity to tell the housekeeper that I didn't inform him that I was going away.

As circumstances would control, while I was still in the US news reached me that he died in Sweden. I wrote to the Swedish Government asking for the death certificate which was forwarded to me.

I was free we were free, free from the conniving, calculated, consistent, selfish, behavioral actions of a deceitful dishonest man.

I remember him taking an easy chair, placing it on the lawn in the sunlight, as he stretched himself out as long as he could, his hair colored in gold with grey strands forcing themselves to breathe and gain some air and escape from the prison of chemical entanglement. Such a life, my dear three boys needed better direction, better examples, a man they could emulate, and the Good Lord worked His Miracles and set us free.

Fourteen

Beautifully Enchanting
Exotic Dominica

My oldest son John graduated from the Adventist Secondary School in Portsmouth, Dominica, and I insisted that he got ready to go to college in the U.S.A. He did not relish the idea of leaving his brothers and me, we were all so very close, but life has many angles, takes many turns and different directions. Life demands we assume meaningful varied ways to proceed towards a positive, satisfying, future. I arranged with his Aunt Ruth, his father's sister to have John live with her so he could attend college, he was eighteen years old at the time; his father was recently deceased; every telephone call I got from John, "mummy, I want to come home," ""John you must study, time will all go by quickly and before you realize it, and you would be through." "But mummy I want to come home" all the time, every time, each time we spoke on the telephone, "mummy I want to come home," I visited Aunt Ruth, Uncle Harry and John. "All John talks about and thinks about is Dominica, you and his brothers," Aunt Ruth said to me, and I noticed that John hardly left me when I was there. Having realized that John was terribly home sick, one day before I returned to Dominica, I said to him, "you can come whenever you want to", and I was back to Dominica. After two weeks, John was back in Dominica camping around with his brothers. He had applied to a school of motor mechanics in Arizona, and he was accepted. Meantime, my second son Kenneth had two more years to complete before finishing high school, while the youngest, Walter Jr. Who was the most eager to go to the U.S.A, he would be graduating from elementary school. I decided therefore that the time was right for a move since Walter Jr. could start high school in the USA. I went to Massachusetts with the hope of enrolling the youngest two boys in an Adventist High school only to be informed that the Adventist High school was in Florida. I flew to Florida. I liked the campus, and the persons who attended to me were very kind and helpful. The school was both a boarding school and a day school. Since I knew no one in Florida and had no one on whom I could rely. An Adventist Boarding school seemed the perfect place but the boys had to vacate the school on weekends. There was more work to accomplish.

When I returned to Dominica, I found in my mail box, a letter for John from the school to which he had applied in Arizona (Arizona is over two thousand miles from Central Florida) informing him that they had a campus in Orlando. Orlando borders Altamonte Springs the general area where my youngest two boys would be attending school. You can imagine our joy and relief. The boys, all three, would be in the same locality, we were thankful to the Almighty and extremely delighted.

The boys were all born at a Boston, Massachusetts hospital but they never ever lived in Boston. They lived their earliest years in Norton, Massachusetts and the younger two started their school years in Dominica, West Indies, with their father and mother present and involved in their daily lives. Dominica was a precious environment where the boys roamed free, climbed trees and played with goats and sheep. A place where their innocent minds directed them to take live chickens running free from in the yard and place them on their clothes closet rod and give those chickens a carpet of their suites and trousers and shirts.

Now daddy was no longer there, he was with his Maker. Our lives had to go on. They were growing up and they had to be educated. We had to face life without daddy, since the schools they would attend were in Central Florida we were in the process of moving to Central Florida. The only thing we knew about Central Florida was that The Florida Institute of Motor Mechanics and Forest Lake Academy were both in Central Florida. You may imagine we were forging on a new experience, a new journey in our lives with great excitement and zeal.

LUCILLE

One day at a church gathering during the period of enrolling Kenneth and Walter at Forest lake Academy, I was extremely fortunate to be seated next to a woman from ST. Lucia/Barbados, one from Jamaica, whom I conversed with, I mentioned that I had come to Florida to register my two sons at Forest lake Academy but I had no idea where the boys would go on weekends as I Live in Dominica and I did not know anyone in Florida. The ladies listened with attention. When I stopped talking, one of the ladies, the younger of the two, who was about forty-to-forty five years old said, "don't worry about that, we will take care of them. We will make sure that they are alright. You do not have to worry, they will be in good hands." I felt the Power of God and how He looks upon his own who trust in Him. I felt a certain affirmation and never doubted that the ladies meant what they promised. I felt certain deep inside of me that they would. I was relieved of a burden a weight of uncertainty, of indecisiveness was lifted off me. God performed His Magic. I could return to Dominica more peacefully ready to continue to formulate plans for keeping the boys at forest Lake Academy.

One has to have faith and a sincere belief in the power of God to observe, understand and appreciate the works of the Divine Master. Circumstances occur which we humans cannot occasion nor control, yet we notice and feel their impact in definite, basic and fundamental ways. When two ladies, take it upon themselves and volunteer their services to assist a woman trying to put two boys in Christian school, a woman whom neither of these ladies knew from anywhere; a total stranger; this has to be the Divine Provision of God. God delivers to those who trust in him and believe in his wonderful works.

He rewards those who do his good works. We should be our brothers keepers; those who do prosper by the grace of the living God; their gains are multiplied, their works are seen. They help others prosper and develop. Communities are upwardly uplifted as a result.

Lucille is blessed by God, this woman was God's angel sent to guard my boys. She looked out for them, she kept in touch with them, she bought them food products that they were accustomed to eat in Dominica, she invited them always to her home, to Thanksgiving Dinner, Christmas etc. she was simply a guardian angel, a marvelous woman, a practicing Christian. Her kindness to those three boys whom she labeled "MY BOYS" was absolutely remarkable, the manner in which, and how good she was to them goes without asking or expecting anything in return; she is one of her kind one would definitely have to be blessed by the Almighty to act like she did. She will not, ever be forgotten. I will remain always grateful to her.

In July 1993 when I took Kenneth and Walter Jr. to Orlando to settle them at their boarding school which would start classes on August 1. I was positive that they would have two friends looking out for their welfare. Once Kenneth was not feeling well, I thought that I should try to have him come visit me for a little while and what did Lucille do? Lucille bought Kenneth a new suit. I imagine that she well knew a jacket suited outfit is something the boys could not afford so she provided him with one so he could visit his mother in style. What thoughtfulness and generosity. Actions of that kind do bring their own reward even in the happiness these people experience while practicing such deeds, these folks are distinguished from other people. Such folks are treasures to society. They make life more pleasant for others, they spread happiness, as a result, families are uplifted, communities develop as a more humane society more able to notice the needs of their neighbors as they live and exemplify the true meaning of the creeds "we are our brothers' keepers". They "do to others as they would have others do to them".

A few years ago I was visiting the boys. I stayed up all night cleaning, washing walls and dusting windows and wiping shutters the night before my departure; on the airplane the following day I was sitting at the isle end of the row, a woman was sitting to the right beside me and we were conversing, pretty soon I fell asleep; when I awoke I apologized to the lady and explained to her that I was sorry for going to sleep while we were talking. I related to her that I lived in Dominica, in the Caribbean and I was visiting my boys who I had in a Seventh Day Adventist School in Florida, and the reason I fell sound asleep is because I never went to bed the night before as I was cleaning the house for the boys. We were speaking again and the lady handed me a small folded paper. I took it thinking it was a candy bar. I opened it to find it was a one hundred dollar bill. I thanked the lady and was handing the money back to her saying she didn't have to do this. "I want you to have it" the kind, generous lady replied, "anyone who works so hard to put her children through a Christian school deserves to be helped" the kind lady said and she closed my hand. I thanked her and realized that I was so very fortunate to meet such thoughtful, kind and generous people. I knew that it was God's intervention. I had spent all my money helping the boys and buying them a few things, I told myself that I did not need much as I would manage in Dominica; between them, the boys had given me twenty dollars. That was all I was returning with to Dominica. Thanks to the dear lady I then had one hundred and twenty dollars. She got off the next stop and we continued on our different journeys.

I was back in Dominica alone, working to keep two young teenage sons in private school and to pay a mortgage in Florida so they could have as much independence that I could provide them. With help of their big brother, and with sacrifice from each one of us, we managed fine. I visited them once a year. I always found them abiding, discrete, respectful, obliging, confident and cooperative, willing to economize. These attributes in them made me more astute in my deliberations, eager and proud to push them to a solid foundation. They were fabulous, simple, dependable, honest and loving. The kind of young men people admired, and they carried these straits of character with them. I have never had any problems with any of them. In this world of turmoil and disgusting behavior on the part of teenagers, I consider myself very fortunate and especially blessed. I live for their personal enrichment, and hope for their self fulfillment. They have given me satisfaction more than I can explain, I couldn't ask for more.

Something I am especially proud of is that they have remained close, brotherly love between them is very evident as they are attuned to the welfare and well being of each other. They are individuals of course as well they should be and live separate lives with varying interests but their sense of cohesion, concern and interest in the workings, interests and doings of each other is very remarkable, attitudes of which they should be very proud. It is not often that young men today sacrifice of their own needs and possessions to ease the wants and burdens of their siblings; habits of suchlike nature are very remarkable indeed and foster their individual and as well as their collective development and progress. I feel very positive that this behavior is for keeps, it is real, that that solidarity will prevail. It reminds me of the time when they were still very young, John was about nine or ten years old and he noticed the way we acted as sisters which prompted him to state to me, "mummy, I hope when we get older that we will be as close to each other as you and your sisters are"

I do sincerely think they have accomplished that possibility and I am happy about it indeed.

BIG BROTHER

I advertised some items for sale on the Dominica Chronicle, John, an ingenuous young man as he always was, was now to handle the selling of the articles while I was away. When I returned to Dominica, to my greatest, amazement and absolute delight, John informed me that he had fifteen hundred (1,500) dollars there awaiting me. Having to pay for three boys' schools and residence in a new city, an environment where we knew no one except two strangers who try to befriend us, you know that the Almighty looks over you and provides your needs.

Now that his two brothers were gone; John was eager to go. He arranged to begin school in September he would have to enroll at his school. His eagerness grew in great intensity. We left in early September. Now that my three sons were in school in Central Florida, that is therefore the place that I should be, right there with them. I arranged for a school principal friend and his family to stay in our home to take charge of things. His father was already working on the farm. I moved to Central Florida. John and I were rooming with an old lady who lived alone. We purchased a vehicle and started house hunting. John, while attending the Institute Of Motor Mechanics also took on a full time and a part time job, you couldn't ask for a more concerned and thoughtful young man, he paid the household bills, and we continued house hunting for a place of our own. When graduation time came, John graduated at the top of his class. He continued working while trying to find new employment in his field of study. We pulled our resources together and paid a down payment on a property with open space and trees in a very quiet, gated, protected residential area, a bicycle riding distance from Forest Lake Academy. The boys were as thrilled as ever you could imagine. They were jubilant, they had never lived in the city and now I was not going to subject them to the city, they would be together sheltered beneath trees, that to which they were accustomed all of their lives. They would not be subjected to a landlord limiting their laughter and movement.

The house was very spacious, four bedrooms, there was a stove, a refrigerator, dish washer, a washing machine, air condition and a swimming pool, and a huge couch which had seen better days. The basic requirements were all in place. Money was tight as one would imagine, I bought a queen size water bed, on which we all four slept. We enjoyed the Jumping Jacks before falling asleep. Furniture, I decided would wait till later. I collected two strong, good sized, cardboard boxes and fitted them tidily with plain tablecloths so the boys would have a place on which to lay their books. Going into additional debt was not an option. They rolled over the carpeted floor and enjoyed their freedom of being under their own roof again free from any landlord limiting their movement or laughter. To say that John was a good boy does not in any way convey the magnitude of that young man, he always was as dependable as one would want an eldest son to be, exemplary to his two younger brothers and very concerned about his mother's whereabouts.

John is almost seven years older than Kenneth, almost nine years older than Walter, and he always amazed me with his ability and his capacity to come down to his brothers' level even when they were very little to afford them joy, companionship, friendship, togetherness, guidance and happiness. At the same time he always stood tall, high above them, not only in height at this stage, but by the examples and the direction he delivered to them. He was a real BIG BROTHER in every sense of the word.

In Moore Park, he worked on the farm, He was the one who overlooked the workers, transported the bananas to the buying station and cleared the farm road. He bought and repaired damaged motorbikes, and sold and rented them out, he was indispensable and ingenuous. Once I got into a motor vehicle accident, the door of my jeep was totally damaged, crushed, completely wrecked. The insurance company wrote the thing off. John all alone, with help from no one, fixed the door. I have no idea how or where he developed his mechanical ability, daddy had all the tools available and John capitalized, and put them to great use. He was immaculate in his work. He fixed the door beautifully and repainted the jeep. It looked like new again. This young boy proved his worth and really amazed me. I never knew he was so capable, so efficient an automobile repair man.

Having THE HOUSE here in Florida to make our new HOME was a landmark for me in my personal development. It was a true achievement. Before that I lived in a house my husband had bought, and before that, I lived with my mother and grandmother in their two side-by-side homes. I had never lived in rented quarters. I did not want my abiding sons growing up in a rental environment and subjected more easily to the ills of society more vulnerable to the pranks of city kids and wayward boys and to have less freedom for their whereabouts. I pulled whatever resources I could command and put a down payment on that house. It was an accomplishment of which I am very proud. I was embarking upon a real estate venture I knew precious little about. Home Owners Management Association, with its added costs and twenty years fixed VA loan. I was not a USA veteran; I have never been in the USA Military. Why a veteran's loan fixed at 9.5% while mortgage loans have been reduced several times to as low as 3 1\2%! I was stuck at 9 1\2 % Fixed! BUT! I was determined and steadfast. My youngest two boys were in Seventh Day Adventist boarding school. This was the happening that took us to Florida. And I sure as anything was going to do all I could to keep them there and also to bring the three of them together under their own roof. I was fortunate to have found this house close enough to the school so the boys could ride their bicycles to school and be independent. We sacrificed. The boys never asked for much, they were dependable, obliging, cooperative, respectful and dutiful. Among the millions of foreclosures people experienced this year alone; my mortgage; my home, my property: is mine, ours, and was not, and won't be; one among the foreclosures; for I am a veteran of my womankind. As I write, I have paid my last mortgage payment and received an escrow refund. Thanks to the cooperation of my sons who helped so we claim that milestone. To accomplish this, I have had to leave the boys in Florida and return to work in Dominica, since after trying and paying employment agencies. I was still unsuccessful, in getting employment. School and the mortgage had to be paid. I would not relinquish. I would not falter. Thanks to the nature of the boys. I could trust them. Their manner, discipline, obedience, respect, character and togetherness, always was beyond reproach. John the big brother, became also "mother" and "father" attending PTA meetings and keeping control and guardianship over his two younger brothers.

I sent money to the boys as often as I earned it. They were very responsible boys who earned my trust and confidence. They adhered to principals and they knew what was important. God directed us. Cable and Wireless, the major telecommunications company in Dominica wanted a suitable place to erect a major antenna in their efforts to establish connections for embarking on the mobile telephone industry. They approached me, we discussed proceedings and because it was a project to facilitate progressive improvements on Dominica, I decided to sell them a small portion of land. Little did I think at the time how appropriate and timely a few thousand dollars would be in our pocket, from the time we acquired Moore Park I have tried to explain to the boys the important role that that place could play in their lives and that they should refrain from selling it as it could provide the collateral for improvement in their economic development. The same day I received the money I wired it all to the boys.

They have all grown up and thank God with dignity, simplicity, respect and character. They have all gravitated in the direction of their boyhood interests.

John had been a bicycle enthusiast in Dominica, a sport in which he still maintains great interest and participates in here in Florida. In 1903 he was elected "Sportsman of The Year". He graduated from the Seventh Day Adventist Secondary School in Dominica, and, at the top of his class at the Institute Of Motor Mechanics in Florida. He is very proficient in repairing motor vehicles, motor bikes, bicycles and other motors.

Kenneth attended Forest lake Academy and obtained his diploma from Seminole Community College. He was eager to begin studies to enhance his boyhood love of building airplanes. As a child he delighted in building model airplanes from tin, paper and cardboard. He was attending Embry Riddle Aeronautical University when I received a call from him sadly explaining that every time he had to study he would get very severe headaches. I did not hesitate, I advised him to withdraw from that course of study as his health and well being should be his primary focus. I am satisfied that he listened and acted accordingly. He still enjoys his affinity to airplanes he has a small collection of planes, and attends airplane shows.

He is a roofer and an enthused finance advocate. He handles my financial obligations, helped to pay the mortgage, keeps all our bills in check and pays them on time.

Walter was the electric magnet, he had to find out what made electrical things work. I had a small portable television radio, almost new designed like a traveling case, one day

I came home to find that Wally had my much liked TV radio pulled apart undergoing his investigations; I was taken aback but I realized that he was feeding his inquisitive mind and interests so I took it all in stride. The unfortunate happening is though that I transferred the boys to Florida soon after before Walter had the opportunity to re-assemble my favorite entertainment item.

When Walter was about nine or ten years old a girlfriend of mine who knew of Wally's interest was experiencing problems working on her electric sewing machine, she called on my telephone "sister Moorhouse do you think Wally could come and see what's wrong with my sewing machine?" "I'll give him the phone you talk to him" "Mummy sister Simon wants to know if you would allow me to go and check her sewing machine it is giving her trouble" "Oh yes of course, go and see if you can help her." Well my little electrician was delighted, he took a screwdriver and he hurried off. Sister Simon lived about one and a half miles away from us, before Wally arrived back home my telephone rang, "sister Moorhouse Wally got the machine working beautifully, I want to thank you" "Don't thank me, thank him" I said to her, delighted as ever, and I congratulated Wally when he arrived. He had a big grin on his face and I knew he was proud of himself and his accomplishment.

After graduating from Forest Lake Academy, Walter attended the ITT Technical Institute he was class valedictorian and shared the stage with officiating personnel.

He then attended The University of Central Florida and obtained a Bachelor's Degree in Electrical Engineering. He is employed as an electrical engineer with Florida Power.

After working for one year Walter purchased his home, he is married and has one son and two daughters. His wife claims he is a wonderful husband and great father whom she loves very much.

Happenings around the world, drugs, greed, envy, selfishness, brutality, bullying, have not impacted upon the lives of the boys. They have remained focused and quite reserved. Once when the younger boys were still in high school I received a telephone call from John, "Mummy", he started, "Kenny came home and told me about a nice looking car which he saw for sale, he said that the price was quite reasonable so I went to check it over. It is a good deal and we would like to buy it." "Well" I replied, "if you think it is a good deal and you can afford it, then buy it" "But mummy I have no money", "well forget about it, you have the Bronco your brothers have their bicycles" "Mummy, Wally has some money" "You boys decide what you want to do and call me back". It is well known that as kids grow and teenagers get close to 'driving age' about the first thing they want is a vehicle, there was one vehicle and Kenneth was approaching driving age. Sometime later that day my telephone rang, it was John. "Mummy we bought the car," "great! Whose car is it?" "Mummy it belongs to all three of us. Kenny saw the car, Wally had the money, and I had to make the decision to buy it". Does a mother so far away across the Atlantic Ocean, who works in Dominica to keep two boys in a Christian School in Florida need more satisfaction? I was deeply gratified, heartily grateful and exceedingly proud of my boys' mentality, togetherness and cooperation. Their father would have been very proud of them.

Their father did not like Florida and I doubt that he would have lived there, but he was gone I wanted my boys to have a Seventh Day Adventist Christian education so we came to where the school was. Walter definitely would want them to be educated and I am positive that he would have been mighty proud of them for the way in which they conduct their lives. He was in his simple way of life an example to them. He loved them dearly and provided for his family as best he could with his meager means. He shone his light on them. As he jokingly uttered that night at dinner to throw a little light on the dark subject, he definitely threw a light upon me, a bright and shining lifelong light which reflects on our children three delightful sons he gave me. He changed my life, he made it better. He gave me a very practical education by noticing him and the things he did, his concern for other people, his unselfishness, his tendency towards the simple life, his enjoyment of nature and his ability to supplement his income by using the wild fruits of nature and growing and processing most foods which the family consumed, enabled his family to travel and enjoy varied forms of entertainment and a good life. I knew that Walter loved me; but like many other men, at some point he strayed, he was engaging in outside affairs with at least one girl. Though he tried to hide his involvement the evidence was clear as some women willingly make their affairs known through various forms of malicious demeaning advertisement.

As a woman who grew up without a father in her life, and because of my love for Walter and the desire that my children would have their father in their home, as one who wanted to maintain the family unit, I confronted Walter head on. I produced some objects from the girl's lucid advertising and informed him that his truant selfish inclinations, his participation and activity in his outside sex affairs could be damaging to the welfare of his boys whom he loved so much, that such behavior could cause the family to split, and would be detrimental to his own happiness. He could hardly face me. He knew I was dead on target and that he could not deny his ugly doings. Walter was a businessman who was often on the road. I could not follow him around. I had no intentions of so doing. He had to come to grips with his life and decide what was better for him and his family. He would be faced with his own decision to do or not to do, to go or to be home, to be daddy to his three sons, or to see them out of his home. Life does not provide easy answers but sometimes we have to be on attack mode when occasions demand it. We should be accountable for our actions and determine which course of action, which direction we take. I am not in any position to know whether Walter curtailed his affairs. When one loses trust it sometimes never is regained. Walter knew that I knew and he knew that I made him aware of what I could do or make happen as a result of his unfaithfulness and deceit. The rest was up to him. Bad habits are hard to break, he was no innocent baby, he knew what the repercussions could be and he knew what he was doing. He seemed to have understood my seriousness. We were family. We had to make decisions, find solutions. I am not a proponent of divorce. I know full well that it is the children who suffer in ways unimaginable. I would try everything I could to keep the family together and as happy as I could.

Personally, I have been very faithful to my husband, in my way of thinking a woman should be a model of exemplary behavior and character to her children and society. It is my belief that a woman should never endeavor to repay her husband's insincerity by being unfaithful and insincere herself. A mother should not attempt to follow a man around and be a free for all, a free agent on call as she degrades herself and becomes shameful to her children and to her community. She should work to establish and maintain a happy home wherein the children copy her and learn the fundamentals and rudiments of building character. Children, boys and girls alike have always had the tendency to emulate their mothers more than their fathers. Motherhood is a state of being experienced by mothers alone, one which should not be taken lightly. Motherhood demands certain modes of behavior; mothers are the cornerstones, on whose shoulders society is built. A wife falls much into the same category. Women in general, we cannot afford to imitate men and practice the same when they graze fields of sexual pleasure. Women should be a different breed in that regard. We should strive for moral servitude and realize that women are mothers to all men and we influence them. Men are not the only culprits either, a stray man finds a willing woman and the act is on. We should be firm in our involvement, committed in resolve, and try to be not easily swayed, to know and decide the straight or narrow path. People's attitudes in life have changed, but life still remains the same, the basic rudiments of life, of being a woman, a wife, of being mother, of being father, these attributes will always be there, they never change, they come with responsibility, they are there for us to deal with, everyone of us, to upgrade, or to demoralize. We should open ourselves, open our hearts and embrace their merits, new visions and pathways of development.

Men should understand that women can also choose to roam. I am of the opinion that that is something which married men would detest, they would not like their wives to be on the loose, they should therefore try to consider that marriage demands an even path, truth, sacrifice, compromise, and steady work to keep each other happy, both spouses owe respect, sensibility, sincerity, faithfulness and honesty to each other, they should work towards maintaining a mutual partnership to entertain and foster happiness in marriage.

Happiness in marriage creates its own path, each couple is different than the other, they have different ideals, and like beauty happiness is in the eye of the beholder, if we work relentlessly, steadfastly to make each other happy, as we should, and strive to achieve a degree of understanding and cooperation, we could make each other enjoy greater happiness. That's what happiness is all about. That's what a happy marriage entails.

Walter once related to me that his friends were all telling him how lucky he was to have such a young attractive woman for his wife, and what they would like to do. In the same breath Walter then very seriously said "you do whatever you want to do just you never let me know about it"

From the time I was in my early teenage years, I had made up my mind that I had to hold the reigns tight. I did during all of my teenage years and all of the years before I got married. I have always been determined in that respect. My husband well knew it. He had nothing to worry about. I was not about to let loose now that I was a married woman. I praise the Lord that by His grace I held the ropes tightly, kept a steady head and kept the doors shut. I have been honest and truthful and I delivered to my husband a faithful sincere one-man's love.

Life continues, we must move forward and tread the path ahead. I have been twice married, twice widowed, two senior white men, one American, one Swedish, both of whom were quite older than me, two ambitious men, one with integrity, one with impunity. Two men who were very different in their manner and deportment, and way of life; the one who worked extremely hard to meet the needs of his family, and the other, a vulture, very inclined to the easy life and make belief determined to live at the expense of other people, and the one who was selfless and assisted any person any way that he could. In life one expects people to be different in their ways, habits, attitudes, their likes and dislikes, their customs, religion and beliefs. One never hopes to find nor expects a man to reap his neighbor, much less exploit his wife, in shadowy carefree, calculated predefined ways. Such behavior leads to bedlam, and destruction and collapse of other people and himself, his wife, his marriage, his family, yet, besides it all, one has to forgive, strive to move forward, live with dignity, character and respect. A mother in so doing dwells not on negative inconsistencies instead she pushes her foot fast forward and overcomes obstacles which would otherwise be detrimental to her progress and the progress and life and well being of her children. She etches a new beginning, a new way of life. Happiness for herself and her children is her goal. We have overcome odds and we know we will face and have to overcome many more, we also know that with discretion, dedication, determination, good will and hard work, opportunities for success lie before us, so we keep striving. We keep trying forward movement, for we know, as it must, that Life continues.